A TRUTH ENLIGHTENS ME PRODUCTION

FINITE OBSTACLES

INFINITE TRUTH

DR. ROB ANTHONY

FINITE OBSTACLES / INFINITE TRUTH
by Dr. Rob Anthony

Copyright © 2022 by Dr. Rob Anthony

All rights reserved. This book or any portion thereof may not be reproduced or used in any manner whatsoever without the express written permission of the publisher except for the use of brief quotations in a book review or scholarly journal.

ISBN: 978-1-7376067-0-3

Printed in the United States of America

Cover and Book Design: Mike Murray, Pearhouse.com

ACKNOWLEDGEMENTS

I must first acknowledge that this book would never have been possible if it were not for my loving savior Jesus Christ. It is the relationship I have been building with him ever since that December evening in 1991 that began this journey of trials that yielded the lessons of which I document in this book. If it weren't for his love and strength, I would be a broken man. If it weren't for his gifts, I would not be able to convey my messages. If it weren't for his conviction, I would be lost. I am forever indebted to the Lord Jesus, and I want my life to be a "living sacrifice" back to him.

I also want to thank my wife, Renee for believing in me. Her encouragement and love has radically changed me into the man I am today. She is the "why" I do what I do.

I also owe nothing but gratitude to my mother, father and two sisters. When I was at my lowest point, they never gave up on me, supported me, and loved me.

I owe much to my grandma Marilyn and late grandpa Frank. I especially appreciate the fact that they were never ashamed of the gospel.

I appreciate my step-son Brandon allowing me to share my wisdom with him. He is such a sharp young man who will accomplish great things in the future.

I also want to thank the staff at Fox High School and Clinton Middle School for their friendships and the opportunity to work with such great professionals. We have impacted hundreds of children's lives due to our willingness to undertake the many challenges that come with being an educator. I salute every one of you.

I am indebted to Morris Morrison for assisting me with getting this book published. It was a forty-five-minute phone call with him that changed my outlook on writing. When I doubted myself, he did not. When I did not know where to start, he did and set it up for me. When my dream wasn't big enough, he brought out the "Morrison Construction Crew" and blew out my narrow walls so I could see a bigger picture.

I am grateful to Mike Murray first of all for his patience with me as a first-time publisher. I essentially learned how to become a published writer on-the-job, and Mike's guidance and direction were invaluable as I went through this process. Mike never said a negative word when I would have to change something, and his patience with me and his expertise have made this book possible. Mike, you are best!

Lastly, Braeden, I love you.

Table of Contents

How to Read This Book vii
Prologue 1
Introduction 9
Go: Be a Conqueror, Not a Camper 13
Not So Fast, My Friend! 19
Botany Can Be Painful. 27
Forget What You've Been Remembering 31
There Are Seven Sage Sirens 37
God's Omniscience Isn't a License to Avoid Prayer 43
Oh!!!! That's Deep! 49
More Than Just a… 55
Get "Un-stuck" in Your Ways 59
Remember. Don't Forget 65
It's Faith, Not Logic 71
You're No Different Than a Doughnut 77
Veritas Lux Mea 83
Don't Envy the Wicked 89
God Sometimes Destroys His Own Altar 95
It's What You Feed Your Mind 101
Remember, Repent, and Return 105
You Are in the Lineup for a Specific Purpose 111
Sometimes It's Their Reaction That Matters. 115
The "Here-There" Principle 121
It's What's in the Jar, Dude 127
Are You Barnabas, Paul, or Timothy? The Answer is "Yes." 133

No Reserves, Retreat, or Regrets..139
Carla Lives!..145
You Have to Die Before You Can Live..151
Take Care of the House...157
Even Storm-troopers Cannot Break the Seal....................................163
Don't Forget to Pray..169
Give God Something to Bless!...175
Strong People Are Forged by Strong Hands.....................................181
Choose Friends, Not Desert Isolation..189
Epilogue...195

How to Read This Book

This book does not have to be read front-to-back like a traditional novel. It has been written in a manner so that the reader could simply go to any of its thirty-one lessons and learn something of value and truth. I specifically included thirty-one lessons in case someone wanted to use this as a devotional book where they read one lesson per day of the month.

I begin each lesson with a passage from the Bible. While there are many sound versions of the Word of God, I simply chose the translation which I believe captures the spirit of the lesson as accurately as possible. Some trained theologians may dispute the versions I chose due to their expertise in the Biblical languages and that is fine. I likely do not have their level of training, and my goal is to record Bible verses that are the easiest for a layman or laywoman to understand from my perspective. This is obviously a subjective issue, but I did my best to ensure the passage was easy to understand while maintaining a sense of relevance with the lesson that follows. None of the versions have been noted, however, for my goal is not to get into a debate over which translation of the original manuscripts is better than the other. I again only sought a translation that offered an opportunity for my readers to understand God's Word so that they can apply it in real-life situations. To me, that is what is of most importance.

I also have included many footnotes for such a small book. Most of these have been inserted with a layperson in mind. When I was a new Christian, I often read or heard people state something from the Bible, and I recognized it as scriptural but did not know the exact location of that statement within the text of scripture. Since I was the type of person who always wanted to "double-check" what was being taught to ensure it was in the proper context found within God's Word, I have attempted to footnote any references I make so that the reader can easily look up that verse(s) in a similar fashion. I became saved long before the Internet made it easy to search out a verse, so I would spend much time scouring through the Bible in an effort to locate what I thought was the right verse. I have attempted to limit that search-time for the reader.

Regarding the footnoted verses, I have chosen to utilize two Bible websites that I believe are helpful. Whenever I quote a single verse in scripture, I always have footnoted a link to that verse within the "Bible Hub" website that can be found here: https://biblehub.com. The reason I chose this site is because it offers all of the available translations of a particular verse right on one page, which enables the reader an easy option of reading a referenced verse in various translations with a click of the mouse. Whenever I have quoted multiple verses in succession, I chose to utilize the "Bible Gateway" website located at: https://www.biblegateway.com. Since the "Bible Hub" site lists all of the available translations for the reader on one page, from what I have been able to determine, it does not have the room to do so for multiple verses. However, the "Bible Gateway" site is able to list the verses in succession as they are found in the Bible while also providing a drop-down box to toggle through the available translations. Essentially, if I footnote a single verse, the website I recorded will take the reader to the "Bible Hub" site of that verse. If I footnote multiple verses, the website I recorded will take the reader to the "Bible Gateway" site of those verses.

Not all footnotes are Bible verse references, but when a direct quote is used, I have footnoted the verse(s) followed by one of the two website links to that verse. My goal was to make this book as user-friendly as possible, and since there is both a tangible book and a virtual book available, I wanted the virtual book-readers to have an opportunity to simply click on the link so that they may access the Bible verse(s) that are footnoted. If I simply want the reader to have the option of reviewing a thought I have recorded within this text, I typically add a footnote for them to confer with the verse(s) to which is generating that thought. There are not links for those, but I have made the Biblical reference available for anyone who would like more assistance with understanding what is written.

I end each lesson with a prayer. It is my goal that these lessons encourage people into action regarding whatever the Holy Spirit lay on their hearts, and my prayers correspond with each lesson and ask the Lord to work in us in ways that allow for such action based on the content discussed. Please feel free to personalize these prayers if you have the desire.

PROLOGUE

In June of 2019, I was with my colleagues in Washington D.C. at a "Model Schools Conference" for educators. One of many of the keynote speakers was author Simon Sinek, who capped off the weeks' worth of sessions. His speech was about something he identified as "Finite Wars versus Infinite Wars." Once I came home and researched more about Sinek, I discovered he had written a book detailing the topic of his speech that day. The primary crux of his speech revolved around the idea that understanding the differences between these two types of "wars" is essential since they each have a unique impact on how victory is perceived.

Sinek defined finite wars as those little battles with which we engage that accomplish a worldly objective with perhaps a tangible conclusion. For example, most of us fight the struggles of life to achieve a paycheck. Some fight the battle of accumulation of money in order to purchase a tangible "thing" we want. Alternatively, countries fight wars with the objective of gaining land, money, influence, etc. Finite wars focus on the attainment of finite things, thus people act and then gain something objective. If I understood Sinek correctly, his message attempted to demonstrate that a focus on winning finite wars will always occur, but he wanted his listeners to understand that a focus on these types of spoils was only temporary, which is also what the messages contained in the Biblical books of Matthew and II Corinthians declare.

On the other hand, Sinek argued that infinite wars are little battles that seem to have a subjective end. His example contrasting the two main ideas was spot-on. Sinek used the Vietnam War as his example. The United States was finitely focused on winning battles, stopping supply lines, taking more casualties than they suffered...all things measured objectively. The Vietnamese, however, (and one could argue Communism on a grander scale) fought a war for survival. The nation suffered substantial objective losses in men, money and equipment yet the *idea* (something subjective and infinite) that drove the Vietnamese people to fight lived on as long as they stayed in the war even while suffering huge losses. A modern-day example of an infinite war is the so-called War on Terror. The United States and some of its allies are focused on eliminating certain threats with the belief (or at least expressed ideal) that these actions will quell or possibly eliminate terror threats against the nation. Americans were sold the idea that defeating the Taliban, Osama bin Laden, and Saddam Hussein will accomplish this. However, our nation defeated the Taliban, eliminated bin Laden and Hussein yet terrorism lives on. Why? Because the idea of "terrorism" is infinite and permanent and cannot be defeated.

America also fought the Soviet Union in the Cold War with the goal of defeating Communism. Trillions of dollars were spent[1] yet the socialist ideal lives on even among some in our very own Congress. You see, Sinek was hinting at the point that infinite wars cannot be fought with finite tools and he was correct. Ideas and ideals are infinite. Neither can be destroyed with finite militaries, finite acts of suppression, reorganization, or even the ultimate end of finitude: death itself.

Ever since the Fall of Man, people have attempted to fight God's infinite and permanent truth with a myriad of finite tools. Men and women, armies, and even nations have come against the truthful Word of God, attempting to destroy it yet the truths contained in the Bible have outlived every one of its attackers. People have attempted to rewrite God's Word, banish it, persecute and murder those who teach it, blaspheme it, and obfuscate it but it lives on because truth is eternal. Acknowledging this allows us to then tap into God's infinite truth, allowing mankind the opportunity to maintain a correct perspective on all of the finite obstacles that hinder us on a daily basis.

When one finally grasps this concept, it begs the question, "Why do we attempt to fight infinite wars with finite tools?" The answer to this reveals mankind's own finitude. We do not have infinite minds therefore we think of finite answers. This is precisely why God tells mankind in the Bible that his thoughts are not our thoughts.[2] An infinite God thinks in a manner that created-man could never hope to grasp due to our finite makeup. However, countless men and women in history have attempted to create finite ways to reach an infinite God. We call these attempts "religion." The historical record is full of examples of finite man doing finite things in an attempt to reach an

---

1 https://www.independent.org/publications/article.asp?id=1297
2 Isaiah 55:8; https://biblehub.com/isaiah/55-8.htm

infinite God. The incredible fact, and what Christians identify as the "good news" (the gospel) is that the infinite and omniscient God knew finite man could never do anything to accomplish an infinite salvation, so infinite God became a finite man to accomplish infinitely what finite man never could do! (You might want to read that again.) The Creator's will was always to reveal his love and glory to his creation, but due to man's sin, there was a chasm that separated man from God. Because of mankind's sin-nature, men began succumbing to finite obstacles. Mankind was hopeless to ever bridge that gap because God's requirements could only be fulfilled by an infinitely true and perfect man. While there are numerous finite wars that have occurred in both the past and present, there has always been one ongoing infinite war occurring between good and evil for the souls of men.

Herein lies a very real problem every person has had to face since the beginning of mankind: Created as finite beings yet with an infinite soul and a mind capable of imperfectly operating in both the finite and infinite realms, how then can man win this ongoing infinite war while playing by God's infinite rules while living (at least for a while) finite, sinful lives? This is where Jesus Christ, special revelation, and faith *must* come into play.

A major problem mankind encounters when addressing this question is our pride. We desire to selfishly control our lives and the finite world around us, so how then can we overcome our naturally occurring selfish desire to be the gods of our own lives? Since all of us are indeed involved in this infinite war between good and evil, we have to rely on infinite truth as our weapon to fight it if we want to both perceive and achieve victory correctly. Since finite man has a sin-nature, it is impossible for him to have a perfect understanding of infinite truths every time. So where do we turn to for one hundred-percent, unadulterated truth that we know is infinite, correct, and can always be counted on? We have no other option than to turn to the only infinite and perfect being that exists, and we identify that person typically as "God." We learn in the Word of God that God identifies himself to mankind in the person of Jesus Christ. So we may then conclude that accurately perceiving victory in this infinite war we all fight and achieving victory over the finite obstacles the world presents can only be found in the person of Jesus Christ.

Once we understand that he is infinite and he thus has an infinite source of truth and facts along with an infinite supply of power to accomplish his will, we can then relinquish our attempts to ultimately control our finite world and decide to rest upon the infinite truths that God has shared with mankind in the structure of a book we identify as the Bible. Understanding that we truly are not in ultimate control relieves us of the stress that comes with the attempts to control. Knowing that we have an infinite, omniscient, omnipotent and loving God who has declared his love for his children helps us to place our own faith and trust in his him. Once this is truly accomplished, we imperfectly yet confidently are free to focus on the "Infinite Wars" to which Sinek referred, and the "Finite Wars" we daily encounter become less important. Finite Wars never become irrelevant while we live on this finite planet, but our time can be better spent focusing on what is more important. I argue that building on an infinite and never-shaken foundation of truth is much more important (infinite) than consistently "chasing our tails" attempting to conquer the next fad, the next lie, or the next popular idea that dominates our media broadcasts for but a short time.

Sinek rightly declared that the important wars are infinite. God also said this in Ephesians 6:12.[3] We do not fight against finite things even though finite tools are often used against us. We fight against spirits and principalities that represent infinitely evil ideas derived from an infinitely evil mind. Jesus Christ himself even advised mankind not to fear the finite man who can put us to a finite death, but to fear the infinite God who can place us in an infinite Lake of Fire.[4] This reveals to us that Jesus, in his human and finite body, understood the superiority of infinite thinking. There truly are grander things out there for man to grasp, and God lovingly and graciously invites us to learn three[5] specific infinite truths from him in order to commune with him forever:

1. God invites mankind to live at peace with him, but he is very deliberate in ensuring us that our efforts cannot accomplish this. Only God's infinite and perfect efforts can perfectly bring about infinite peace, and all we have to do is accept them to gracefully receive this peace.

2. God also invites mankind to learn from him. Sinek is onto something here when he argues that infinite ideas are much more important to

---

3   https://biblehub.com/ephesians/6-12.htm
4   Cf. Matthew 10:28; https://biblehub.com/matthew/10-28.htm
5   For a more detailed analysis of "The Three Invitations of Christ," see the article by Billy Graham at https://decision-magazine.com/the-three-invitations-of-christ/.

chase than finite ideas, and the important, infinite ideas *can* be learned because there is one who always is, was, and shall be[6] who has told us the infinite truth. Furthermore, he also promises us his spirit once we are saved, who will teach us and remind us[7] of the important infinite ideas upon which we should focus.

3. A third invitation mankind receives from God is the opportunity to live and dwell with him under an eternal security blanket of sonship.[8] What does a child receive from a parent? Those benefits certainly differ when considering a finite and imperfect parent, but the infinitely perfect parent – God the Father – affords his children a new nature capable of living righteously, a permanent residence, comfort, security, wisdom, affection, love, a just desire to do what is right, and correct discipline to rightfully guide us among other gifts.

Our ability to live both finitely and infinitely in our minds is perhaps part of what God meant when he declared that humans were "made in our ('his' – plural) image."[9] Infinite God wrapped himself in finite flesh in the form of the man Jesus Christ, and for thirty-three years he operated on earth at times in finite ways while always speaking infinite truth.

What do I mean when I state that Jesus "operated in finite ways?" One example in when Jesus ate fish to sustain his finite metabolism. He healed real, objective, handicapped body parts even though they would one day cease to live. He had a finite, objective headquarters in Capernaum from which he handled his three-year ministry. However, he also operated on earth with an infinite purpose, which among many infinite end-goals included the destruction of all that is currently finite and cursed by the Fall of Man.[10] By sitting and eating fish with men, he expressed his infinite love to those with whom he sat. By sitting down with these men, pouring his life and wisdom into them as he shepherded them, he also revealed aspects of his infinitely loving heart toward them. By healing finite limbs, his infinite purpose of love was again revealed. His infinite character of concern for his creation "was exposed" to mankind by his finite

---

6 Cf. John 1:1-3 & 14-15, 8:58, 18:6; Isaiah 44:6; Revelation 22:13; Exodus 3:14
7 John 14:26; https://biblehub.com/john/14-26.htm
8 Cf. Psalm 91:1
9 Genesis 1:27; https://biblehub.com/genesis/1-27.htm
10 Cf. Revelation 21:1

walk as the God-man in flesh. His infinite purpose paying the heavy penalty for mankind's' sin was paid when Jesus died on a finite Roman cross. Most importantly, his finite death on that cross had infinite implications. Finite sacrifices in the old Mosaic system could never take away the infinite sins of mankind against a holy God,[11] so infinite God provided infinite "himself" as an infinite sacrifice for the curse of sin. The way for finite man to be reborn into a new infinite life of the Holy Spirit and eventually receive infinite bodies at our resurrection just as Christ did was an infinite miracle on this finite planet. Again, when Sinek alluded to the importance of infinite wars, I wonder if he knew that he was alluding to Biblical truth?

On that June day in 2019, I couldn't help but think to myself that Sinek's message was no different than the one that the Lord had revealed to mankind many years ago in the Bible. Both Matthew 6:19-20 and I Timothy 6:17-19 advise mankind that a focus on finite components of this earth is unwise because everything finite ultimately has a short shelf-life and will eventually one-day pass away. Additionally, II Corinthians chapter four contains a message from the apostle Paul concerning the affliction he and his contemporaries were suffering due to their evangelism, but after explaining why the suffering he faced was good from God's perspective, the apostle clearly gives us the reason why he could make such a shocking comment. Verses seventeen and eighteen[12] direct us to the fact that being able to distinguish the differences between that which is finite and that which is infinite is important due to the temporary character of those things finite and the permanence of all things infinite. The "seen" we know is objectively observable and finite, and the Lord instructs us that the "seen" is temporary. Much of what we observe and confront in life can thus be relegated as "Finite Obstacles." On the contrary, what is "unseen" is eternal and therefore infinite in purpose. This essential and enlightening "unseen" thing can be identified as "Infinite Truth."

Being able to gain this perspective in life assuredly impacts the way we handle everything that we experience in life. When we can identify finite obstacles and view them as they are, we can then combat them properly. Knowing and then applying infinite truth gives us an invincible weapon to

---

11 Hebrews 10:1-14; https://www.biblegateway.com/passage/?search=Hebrews+10%3A1-14&version=NIV

12 "For our light and momentary troubles are achieving for us an eternal glory that far outweighs them all. So we fix our eyes not on what is seen, but on what is unseen, since what is seen is temporary, but what is unseen is eternal." – II Corinthians 4:17-18; https://www.biblegateway.com/passage/?search=2%20Corinthians%204:17-18&version=NIV

combat finite obstacles because something infinite and eternal will always trump something finite and temporary. This is at the core of God's message to mankind, and I think Sinek understood this when elaborating on his premise. Both the Bible and this book urge us to put our hope in the infinite God because he *is* the "unseen" and infinite truth. He is able to defeat all of the finite obstacles in our paths because his weapon is infinite truth. When the light of truth is shined on darkness, we can see life clearly and appropriately. Once we see clearly, we then understand that the trials we face and our accompanying selfless acts of righteousness amidst those trials build a permanent foundation for the infinite life that is to come. If we allow the Lord to bring us to this appropriate perspective, we will then have the correct perspective of victory as we battle our way through this finite life, for we are then able to maintain our focus on that which is eternal and permanent.

INTRODUCTION

Proverbs 4:18-19 sets two ways before mankind: One way is a path of shining light that continues to grow brighter as we move forward in life and ultimately culminates in eternal life with Christ. The other path is one of darkness that prevents a person from even recognizing that upon which he has stumbled. This path too is ultimately eternal, but it results in eternal death, which Biblically means permanent separation from God. Due to the fact we humans live on a fallen world encompassed by imperfect people who are each influenced by a sin-nature, there will always be many obstacles in our life-journey. Some of those obstacles will be self-created;[13] some will be other-created;[14] and some will simply occur out of circumstance.[15] Light is what enables us to see not just the obstacles inhibiting our way, it also illuminates the flaws we have that need to be corrected. An unpretentious example of this would be if both of my shoe laces were tied together, it would be difficult for me to walk safely. If I attempt that walk in utter darkness, perhaps I could detect that my shoes laces were tied together by the pressure of resistance when attempting to stride. Perhaps I may not be able to determine by feel. Even if I could tell that a knot was in my shoes laces, attempting to unloose a knot in the dark would be difficult and frustrating. My progress would certainly be slowed. However, if a bright light were to be shone all around me, it would not only inform me of what the problem is, it would also enable me to be able to tackle the problem since I could see it clearly. I may struggle going through the process of untangling the knot, but due to the light, I could tell myself to be patient as I work through the untangling. Once the problem is overcome, I could then again progress forward.

Darkness prevents us from focusing on a goal, and it is in fact identified as "the dominion/power/control of Satan."[16] It increases our chances of

---

13   Cf. Proverb 11:3, 19:3; II Timothy 4:10
14   Cf. Genesis 4:1-16, 37:1-36; Nehemiah 5:7-8; Mark 6:14-29. There are many, many more Biblical and personal examples one can reference for problem created for us by other people.
15   Cf. Acts chapter 19
16   Various versions of Acts 26:18 reveal that darkness can be all three. See https://www.biblehub.com/acts/26-18.htm

getting sidetracked. It can put us into dangerous situations that we can't even recognize that we are truly in. Darkness is scary due to the subsequent feeling of the unknown. That fear also causes some to slow down in their efforts and some to freeze-up altogether, thus greatly hindering or completely halting progress. The Bible tells us that the Christian life is a race,[17] and I can't imagine trying to run a marathon in the dark. Yet, many of us choose to do exactly that when it comes to being able to see and then understand spiritual truths. We all inevitably must choose one of the two paths laid out before us.[18]

This brings me to the reason why I have been called to write this book. God has had an infinite plan for my life (and yours too) even before I was conceived.[19] My finite life has, like many of my reader's lives, been extremely difficult and even more revealing of major personal flaws. The Bible informs us that these flaws derive from a "sin-nature."[20] As a result of that sin-nature into which I was born, I have suffered through the loss of children, separation from a child, a loss of dignity, loss of financial security, and I am currently battling cancer and its accompanying feelings of powerlessness. I have suffered through divorce. Many of my dreams have gone unfulfilled. Over time I have realized that I made numerous decisions that were not in-line with my beliefs, and as a result, I have suffered for such decisions. As I age and fight through the treatments of cancer (which are often worse than the cancer itself), my finitude has become very real to me. All of us come to the point where we recognize our humbling finitude. Some graciously experience it at a young age and have a greater part of their lives on earth to seek the infinite truths found in the author of truth, Jesus Christ. Once a person learns these infinite truths, they can adjust their lives accordingly, paying careful attention to that which is infinitely important as the "Light of the world"[21] himself illuminates our way. Some of us do not recognize how feeble our finite lives are until much later in life, and we may feel pressed for time to attend to infinitely important matters. I fall somewhere in the middle of these two categories, and I am thankful that God has called me to offer thirty-one examples from my own life that can help others see finite examples from life that have infinite applications of truth.

---

17 Cf. Hebrews 12:1; II Timothy 4:7; Galatians 5:7; Habakkuk 2:2; Isaiah 40:31
18 Cf. Deuteronomy 30:19-20; Joshua 24:15; John 10:10; II Peter 3:9; Romans 6:23
19 For a list of scriptures that discuss God's plans for humans before they were born, see: https://www.openbible.info/topics/gods_plan_for_us_before_birth.
20 For a list of Bible verses about mankind's sin nature, see https://www.openbible.info/topics/sinful_nature.
21 Cf. Isaiah 42:6; John 1:4 & 9, 3:19, 8:12, 9:5, 12:35-36 & 46; Luke 2:32

Likewise, I also point out at the conclusion of each of these thirty-one stories the finite obstacles that I had to first identify and then overcome to achieve an infinite perspective concerning victory during these trying moments. Due to having to go through each of these personal stories, I learned and want to share that perhaps the most important infinite war we currently face in our nation and around the world is a battle for truth and light.

I will conclude this introduction with a lesson I learned from a beloved friend and colleague in Arnold, Missouri. Her name is Gina, and she has lived through a great tragedy yet done it very well. Her teenaged son, Cole, was tragically killed in a motorcycle accident within feet from her house. In fact, both she and her husband were the first to arrive at the scene of their own son's accident. She obviously took some time off of work to grieve, but when she returned, she once expressed to me in conversation that "everyone has a story." At the time, her statement struck me as a pithy way for a hurting woman to alleviate her sorrow. However, over time and upon deeper contemplation, I realized that she had grasped an infinite truth and expressed it in simple terms. She was right. Every one of us *do* indeed have a story to tell[22] and we should do so, for in the telling we recognize our finitude while at the same time realizing God's infinite purposes we encounter in life. Additionally, when we self-reflect and have the courage to share our story, this allows us to relate with others in authentic ways. Gina is able to connect with grieving parents who have lost a child in ways that no one other person who hasn't suffered through that pain could. I admire her for her strength and the fact that she never let go of God despite such a tragic event occurring in her life. My hope is that as you read these thirty-one finite events that express infinite truths, perhaps some of you will be able to learn authentic lessons just as I did from Gina. Even more, my ultimate hope is that you will begin to discover that Jesus Christ is miraculously revealed to you on a daily basis as you walk through your own finite life-stories, and these revelations of his providence in your life will lead you to seek a saving relationship with him.

---

22 For more information about how my friend Gina has used her own personal and tragic story for infinite purposes, please go to https://www.coleshopefoundation.org/.

LESSON 1

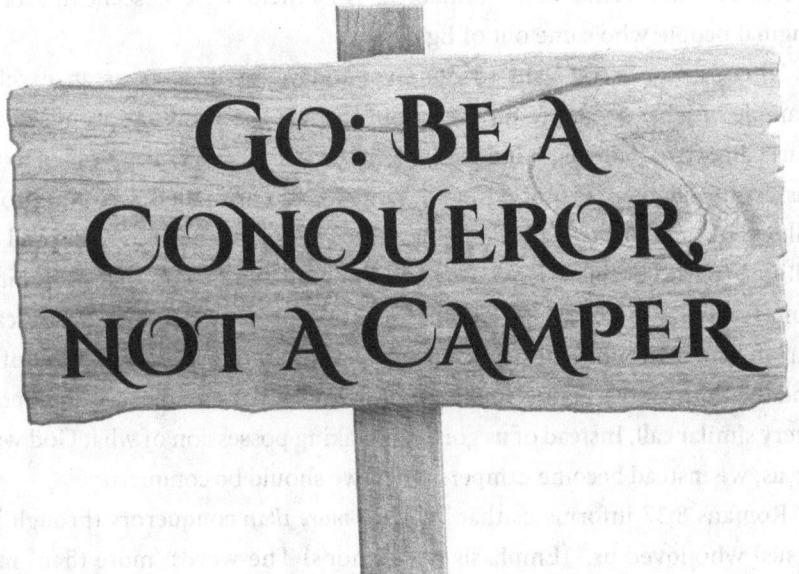

"Go through the camp and tell the people, 'Get your supplies ready. Three days from now you will cross the Jordan here to go in and take possession of the land the LORD your God is giving you for your own'."

JOSHUA 1:11

I chose to use this passage from Joshua for my first lesson because this verse begins with the action verb "go." The writing of this book admittedly represents a big "go" step for me. I spent many years knowing I needed to publish, but I instead decided to linger in the background and watch others do what God also called me to do. Just as the Lord wanted me to "go" and write, he also gave the command to "go" to Joshua, the new leader of the Israelites who had succeeded Moses. The Israelites were at that time camping in the desert wilderness of the Sinai Peninsula and had been for forty years. Of the Israelites that had left Egypt and made the miraculous crossing of the Red Sea,[23] only Joshua and his friend Caleb remained. All others were descendants of the original people who came out of Egypt.

This passage is relevant to our lives today, for it gives us an excellent example of what we are to do because of the fact that God has promised each of us Christians a life of abundance in Christ. The Israelites were called to take possession of their "Promised Land," and we too are called according to the fullness of the Lord to do what he has gifted us to do, and those gifts and that calling are irrevocable.[24] However, one thing many of us do that prohibits us from receiving the blessings God has in store for us is that we tend to "camp out" in our own wildernesses. God told Joshua to "go take possession of the land the Lord God is giving you for your own," and often times we do not heed a very similar call. Instead of us going and taking possession of what God wants for us, we instead become campers when we should be conquerors.

Romans 8:37 informs us that "We are *more than* conquerors through him (Jesus) who loved us." (Emphasis the author's) The words "more than" mean we are even something greater than just a conqueror; we are in fact children of the living God.[25] When people camp, they sometimes go out and make semi-permanent monuments of their presence in an area away from their given habitat. I can remember two summers when I was in 7th and 8th grade when my father and I drove to a New Mexican desert to assist with some archaeology work on an isolated mesa with a professor from Southern Methodist University. I remember very vividly that after a long day's work of digging and sifting, I and many other people there for the one-week period would use a stick to etch into the sandstone rocks a permanent message. Some simply wrote their names; others wrote a message along with the date it was written. Unless those stones are gone, a monument from the past was permanently made in that desert, but we all left that area and went back to our daily lives.

We must be careful in our earthly walk that we do not create monuments upon which to simply dwell. People who "camp out" in life can get so comfortable in their unnatural surroundings – surroundings that God provides for a break but not a permanent dwelling place – that all they do is make monuments

---

23 Cf. Exodus chapter 14
24 Romans 11:29; https://biblehub.com/romans/11-29.htm
25 Cf. Deuteronomy 14:1; Romans 8:16, 9:8

to remember the past and they fail to take action and "go." When we choose monuments over movement, we dishonor God, do not lay claim to the prize before us, and miss out on God's intended blessings for our lives because we choose to camp rather than conquer.

Monuments are often created to honor the dead. In your Christian walk, there will be many "dead" things you encounter. Baptism is an example of a "go" action we do that refers back to a dead thing in our lives. Once we accept God's salvation, the old, dead "you" in sin has passed away, and all things are new,[26] including a new nature that is capable of pleasing God. Baptism is just an outward sign of the inward covenant that has occurred upon that second birth. When a Christian enters the baptismal water, it represents his old self. When he is submerged under the water, this is representative of us dying to our old ways and being buried with Christ, who overcame sin. When that person arises back up out of the water, this is symbolic of our Christian conversion, for we arise from sin due to a new birth because of Christ's death on the cross which paid the sin-debt once for all.[27] It is a real, invisible truth that we were once dead in our sins, but now that we have accepted Christ, we are born again into a new body of Christ. This invisible truth becomes more and more visible to us as we continue to grow in life and "do" things that honor the Christ who gracefully gave us a new birth. We are only able to "do" pleasing things because of that new nature.[28]

We also need to be sure, however, that we remember the "dead" parts of our lives, but we shouldn't dwell on them like a camper. My first marriage occurred, but it is dead now because I am divorced. I am thankful for the experience, but I do not dwell on it day-by-day and continue making new monuments for it. When something dies, you honor it (monuments honor the past) and then you bury it. When something is buried, it should not be dug back up. Burying the dead things in our lives requires us to leave them behind, move forward, and "go and take possession" of the new blessings that are before us.

Digging up dead things always yields an encompassing stench. One example of this is bitterness. Bitterness is a stench that, just like a foul-smelling dead body, makes people leave its presence in a hurry. Another is unforgiveness carried in our hearts. Harbored and ungodly anger also stinks. There are many

---

26 II Corinthians 5:17; https://biblehub.com/2_corinthians/5-17.htm
27 Cf. Galatians 3:13-15; Ephesians 1:7; I John 2:2; Hebrews 9:12 & 22
28 Romans 8:8-9; https://www.biblegateway.com/passage/?search=Romans+8%3A8-9&version=TLB

other forms of stench that occur in peoples' lives when they fail to bury the dead past of their lives and instead are complacent and build monument after monument for their dead. This behavior serves to keep us "camped out" among the stench of the hurtful, dead past. We should instead choose movement toward our promised land once we build a monument over our dead past. Honor those in your past who have hurt you and then bury them. Thank God that your past enemies have helped you draw closer to him. If appropriate, thank them for their contribution to your life. Many of us have developed stronger lives because someone in our past became a thorn in our side, which made us more reliant upon the sufficient grace of God.[29] Some come to the Lord because of previous troubles. God works out all things for the good of those who love the Lord and are called according to his name,[30] and "all things" includes your enemies and the hurt they caused you.

Choose to go. Choose movement, not monument. Choose to conquer rather than to camp. Take the painful, dead events of your life and bury them. Don't dwell on the past, but never forget the past, for it is what God has used to bring you to where you are today. At the beginning of every school year, I always tell my classes, "The only thing worse than nostalgia is amnesia." I then would ask my students to explain what that phrase means, and this lesson always resulted in good debate. Learn from your past and then make a decision to move forward. It is only then, through faith, that God can take you to the promised land he has for you.

FINITE OBSTACLES

Laziness, Uncertainty; Nostalgia, Hurtful events from our lives, Bitterness

INFINITE TRUTH

We are more than conquerors over finite obstacles in life once we are in Christ.

---

29 Cf. II Corinthians 12:7-10
30 Romans 8:28; https://biblehub.com/romans/8-28.htm

Prayer

Dear Lord, I thank you for our past experiences and your omniscient hand that guides us. Thank you for promising to walk through our experiences with us. Thank you for your grace, and thank you for giving us the gift of forgiveness. Please strengthen us to forgive our enemies, bury our dead and to move forward in life. In the name of Jesus, amen.

Lesson 2

"A wise person will understand what to do, but a foolish person is dishonest."

PROVERBS 14:8

For years, I have read this verse and took it at face value. It spoke to me enough that I have it highlighted in my Bible, but as many of us who walk with the Lord learn, the same verse we read year after year can take on new meaning once the Holy Spirit enables us to see it differently when he exposes his infinite wisdom. That is the case with this verse for me. For years I believed that "a wise person will know what to do" due to the fact that they are wise. This is known in logic as circular reasoning, but I didn't know that for many years. My thinking went like this: "Of course a wise person will know what to do in certain situations because they are wise...duh." I can even recall asking the Lord on one occasion after re-reading this verse why he allowed these words to be penned since they seemed to me to be self-evident. I also had a misunderstanding of what it took to acquire wisdom. I once believed that wisdom simply took years of life in order to attain, but I discovered that was not a truthful belief, and I was therefore foolish due to my own self-deception. Once I had the opportunity to go through a very trying time in my life, this was when the Lord taught me by using a phrase made famous by former coach and ESPN college football personality, Lee Corso.

Whenever Coach Corso is giving his Saturday morning commentary on how he believes the next big college football game will occur, he usually states some statistics that support a certain narrative he leads the viewers to believe on the broadcast. After leading the viewers down a path to what seems to be a self-evident conclusion based on the information he presents, he then changes the narrative at the last second by interjecting the comment, "Not so fast, my friend." He then changes up the anticipated result with an upset prediction most would not have expected given what he said leading up to his famous interjection. During my background research of this simple proverb, I began to discover new applications, almost as if omniscient God was gently pointing out the folly of my simple-minded interpretation. I had for many years thought I'd reach the same aforementioned self-evident assumption, but like Lee Corso, further study of the Bible reveals that the Lord too can also answer us with a "Not so fast, my friend."[31]

I once thought wisdom and becoming a "wise person" was a lot easier than it is, and like Lee Corso, the Lord finally had to teach me to think beyond what appears to be expected. As stated earlier, I always thought we gain wisdom just by being alive and going through many experiences. However, what I have discovered is that wisdom is not something that comes to us naturally. Call me naïve; call me what you will, but "wisdom" is a simple term but can only be gained by complex life-experiences. Wisdom is built on a foundation of information one attains before those life-experiences occur and is constructed only when an application of that knowledge is utilized when the opportunity to use it presents itself. That was a long and complicated definition, so I encourage you to read that again. Indeed, gaining wisdom requires time and experience, but time and experience alone does not make one wise. That time

---

[31] I would argue I Corinthians 3:18-19 is the "official" way God sometimes chooses to call us out in our folly.

and experience must be accompanied by information and opportunity in order for it to have a chance to give birth to wisdom. Understanding this concept can help us see why many of the difficult challenges we face are allowed to occur. God wants his children to become informed and wise, but he knows that without being exposed to information first and then giving a person the opportunity to apply that information, a person will not be able to gain true wisdom. The Holy Spirit was given to us to teach us and guide us.[32] As we go through our lives, the Holy Spirit will use all kinds of experiences to teach us something. Also, as we are guided through life, sometimes the Spirit will guide us into situations[33] that allow for us to apply what God has taught us with the end-goal of growth toward wisdom in mind.

A personal example from my life is the three-plus year struggle I've had fighting cancer. I do not know why I got cancer and neither do the doctors according to their own admission. When it was first discovered, I was 45 years old, so I had over four decades of knowledge built up for this situation. God had taught me over the years that I needed to trust him, but saying one trusts and actually doing it are two very different things. I had told the Lord before that I trusted him, and at the age of forty-five, he gave me yet another opportunity to prove it. I knew from Ezekiel 37:1[34] that God does lead us by his Spirit, and he sometimes leads us to a "valley of bones." A valley of bones is a place of death, and cancer certainly can be a place of death. I also knew that from Matthew 4:1[35] that the Holy Spirit even led our Lord Jesus Christ into the wilderness to be tempted by the devil. If God would choose to lead his own perfect son into an arena of temptation, then I would be foolish to think that God wouldn't do the same for one of his adopted sons like me. Lastly, I also knew that Jesus himself told us that we would face many trials in life, but amidst those trials, I should "take heart" because Christ himself overcame those trials.[36] So at the age of forty-five, I was brought to a place where I would face cancer and the temptation not to believe God's Word while going through the struggles, but also an opportunity to come out on the back-end of cancer wiser and more like Christ. While I am not yet totally free of cancer, I can firmly say that I have learned the wisdom of Hebrews 10:35. I have been tempted to "throw away

---

32 Cf. Nehemiah 9:20; John 14:26; I John 2:17
33 Compare Matthew 4:1, Mark 1:12, and Luke 4:1
34 https://biblehub.com/ezekiel/37-1.htm
35 https://biblehub.com/matthew/4-1.htm
36 John 16:33; https://biblehub.com/john/16-33.htm

my confidence" in God, but I have not. I can firmly declare that I have learned the wisdom of Romans 12:12, where I can continue to rejoice in the Lord even while fighting cancer, and I have been "patient in tribulation" and continued praying and waiting for the Lord to do his work in my life. I have learned the wisdom of James 1:2-4 since I have met trials "of various kinds," knowing that "the testing of my faith produces steadfastness (in God)" and that once God is completely done with me on this earth, I will "be complete, lacking nothing." What I am trying to convey is that when a person goes through a serious trial like cancer, he or she is being given the opportunity to grow in wisdom. Our verse above states a "wise person will know what to do," and I admit that when I was diagnosed with cancer, I didn't really know what to do. However, I did have a foundation of God's Word I had learned that taught me to maintain hope regardless of what the doctors said. I also admit that sometimes God chooses to heal sick people and sometimes he chooses not to. Regardless of what he may choose to do in my life, I can affirm that I have become wiser through the process, and I can now help others who are going through the same trials.[37]

So what does the second half of today's verse have to do with me? Similar to how I thought the first half of this verse was self-evident, the latter half also had appeared at first as something self-evident, obvious, and probably not really needed in the Bible. Yet, God graciously has taught me that his methods are much more complicated than my silly mind once thought, and I had to come to a place where I admitted that I wasn't being honest with myself. I may not be alone in this way of thinking, and this could be why God added the second half of this verse concerning dishonesty. The second half declares "a foolish person is dishonest." Dishonesty results in deception. I once thought that this part of the verse implied yet another face-value concept: that a fool lies. Once again, my thoughts were, "Duh." However, a foolish person is indeed dishonest to others, yes; but even more detrimental is that a fool is also dishonest to himself. Once we learn the right thing to do (whether it is reading the Bible, exercising for better health, spending money wisely, etc.) we must begin taking the necessary steps to understand and then apply it. When we fail to apply truth, we actually lie to ourselves. When we give excuses in an attempt to justify our hesitancy, we lie to ourselves. When we procrastinate, we deceive

---

37 Cf. II Corinthians 1:3-4

ourselves. When we do not take God at his word, we are in effect calling him a liar and thus deceive ourselves, sin, and bring shame on ourselves. When we tether ourselves to lies, we move in the opposite direction of wisdom because wisdom can only come from truth.

So what is it that makes us wiser? The experience of cancer did not make me wiser. In fact, I would argue that the experience of cancer can easily make someone bitter. What did make me wiser can be found in the second half of the verse above. The wisdom I gained had something to do with honesty and truth, and who is honest and true? Jesus is. Seeing the truth clearly must occur for us to gain wisdom, for wisdom cannot occur if it is tethered to lies. I John 5:20 gives us insight on what that truth is and how we gain understanding, and I Corinthians 1:30 explains what wisdom is for us. We become wiser when we learn more about Christ. We learn more about Christ by study and by application of that study through trials. Christ came "to give us understanding so that we may know he is true." The Lord has also "been made wisdom unto us." So what truly makes us wiser is the strengthening of our knowledge of Jesus Christ as we undergo trials that tempt us to focus on self rather than him. Prior to my cancer, I looked for wisdom in experiences, but God said, "Not so fast, my friend." Once he gained my attention with this Lee Corso-like interjection, I was then able to see wisdom as it truly is. Jesus Christ himself is wisdom and truth, and we gain wisdom as the Lord Jesus lives his life through us. The experiences we face are opportunities to learn more about Christ, and as we learn more about Christ, we get the side-benefit of learning more about ourselves as well!

In summary, a wise person knows Christ, and as Christ lives his life through the Christian, that person then should take the knowledge they gain from God's Word and use it when opportunity presents itself. From my own experience, I believe God will make sure we get plenty of opportunities to apply our knowledge in life. Once inside those opportunities, we need to make sure we being are honest with ourselves and others so that in our application of truth, we take honest steps towards our problems. We can spend the time in prayer, research and study on the front end, trust that the Lord blesses our honest efforts, and then make a decision and apply it. We should only then look back to self-evaluate so that we may learn from any mistakes made. We are wise because we do not lie to ourselves about the truth contained in God's Word. This allows us to operate in honesty and truth. We can lie to ourselves when we think we are bigger than our problems.[38] We lie to ourselves when we are scared.[39] We lie to ourselves when we suffer from self-doubt and a lack of motivation.[40] The wise person is wise not because of self but because of the Holy Spirit inside him who grants wisdom. It is God's mind that is truthful and honest. It is God's power that is truly bigger than our problems. It is Satan who gives a spirit of fear. It is the power of the Holy Spirit that enables us to overcome self-doubt and a lack of motivation sometimes derived from fear. Indeed, a wise person *will* know what to do because only a wise person will have the Holy Spirit dwelling inside him for Christ was made unto us wisdom.[41] A person naturally doesn't "know" what to do on their own, which is why we are taught. We are wise and know because the author of truth who is wise above all is living his life through the Christian. The fool rejects God[42] and therefore the spirit of God who could be living inside that person, teaching him all things.[43] By rejecting God, a person deceives himself, for he rejects the source of all truth and wisdom and prevents it from residing within him.

FINITE OBSTACLES

Lies, The Unknown, Doubt in God's word, Fear, Trials

INFINITE TRUTH

True wisdom can only come from a knowledge and relationship with Jesus Christ, who has been made wisdom unto us.

---

[38] Cf. Psalm 121:1-8
[39] Cf. Joshua 1:9; II Timothy 1:7
[40] Cf. Ephesians 1:3-6
[41] I Corinthians 1:30; https://biblehub.com/1_corinthians/1-30.htm
[42] Psalm 14:1; https://biblehub.com/psalms/14-1.htm
[43] Cf. John 14:26

PRAYER

Dear Lord, you are bigger than all of our problems and wiser than all of our wisest people put together. People do not wake up in the morning and look at themselves in the mirror and wish to be ignorant, but many of us act in ignorant ways because we do not tap into the source of wisdom: You. Help us to be mindful that the reverent fear of you is the beginning of knowledge. Help us to understand that your Holy Spirit is what teaches us the wisdom we need to successfully navigate this troubled world. Help us to use the gifts and talents you have given us to honor you so that we may act wisely and represent ourselves and you in an admirable way. In Jesus' name, amen.

LESSON 3

*"I have good plans for you, not plans to hurt you.
I will give you hope and a new future."*

JEREMIAH 29:11

Like many home-owners, my wife Renee and I have some bushes planted in the front of our home. I have personally observed my beloved wife give attention to those shrubs over the years, and one morning the Lord used one such observation to communicate application of his Word to me. We have two particular shrubs that just seem to be resistant to flourish. They are stunted in their growth when compared to identical bushes around them that were planted at the same time. However, each year, when it appears those two bushes are going to die, Renee masterfully prunes them and they grow vibrant, green leaves and begin to reflect the beauty they were created to manifest. These shrubs though, do not do so until Renee inflicts temporary "harm" onto the stems that are dead by cutting them off.

This is what God does to us as well. He prunes the dead foliage off of us so that we may grow and become what we were created to become.[44] While I'm not a botanist, I can affirm that plants cannot speak and I believe plants probably do not have a nervous system that "feels" pain. Yet, if we imagine that they do, we can pretend that they also could be angry at Renee for inflicting the "pain" of cutting off the dead stems in order to yield life anew. Nevertheless, Renee does this with a plan for them in mind. She knows that those shrubs will not become vibrantly green and emerge unless she "inflicts the pain" of pruning.

Since I am a human being, I have many flaws. We could think of those flaws as dead stems similar to those found on a bush. One such dead stem that the master botanist (God) had to cut off of me was my pride. When I was a young man, I was overly confident just as many of us are. In fact, I have joked with colleagues that between the ages of thirteen through twenty-nine, I was the "smartest" person on earth. I had all of the right answers, and if you didn't believe that, all you had to do was ask me and I would have told you. I usually continue that self-deprecating story among my colleagues with a truth-statement though. I tell them that around the age of thirty, all of that "knowledge" I once had suddenly escaped my brain, and I finally realized that I didn't know much. While this story is stated tongue-in-cheek, there is some veracity to it. I did suffer with pride. I did think I knew much more than I really did, and at the age of twenty-nine, I went through a divorce. It was during this trying time in my life when God took out his "heavenly shears" and began cutting away many of my dead stems. The process was painful, but once God removed those stems from my life, it was only then that new life could blossom forth. Those blossoms started to bud around the age of thirty for me.

This is the point where our verse and this story merge. We have to trust that God does know what he's doing when we experience the pain from his pruning. We have to stand firmly on Jeremiah 29:11 which informs us that God has "good" plans for us, that he does not want to "hurt" us, and that the goal of his pruning is to give us a "hope and a future" where we fulfill the plans he has for us. But, oh, how hard it is for our sin-riddled and fickle hearts to

---

44 Cf. John 15:2-6 & Hebrews 12:6

trust amidst life's pains and disappointments. If only we took the position of the shrub, where we simply allow God to remove the dead parts of us in order to impart life!

God intends to take care of his creation,[45] even the seemingly inconsequential and commonplace birds like sparrows. However, mankind was uniquely created in God's own image[46] and was the only part of creation for which Christ died.[47] If he was willing to follow through with the atrocities of the Roman cross even for the sinner, how much more good does God have planned for those who accept Christ and become his children? Jesus himself spoke of this concept in Matthew 7:7-12.[48] Let us today repent of our stubborn failure to trust our omniscient Father and reassert our commitment to trust him when he prunes away worthless aspects of our lives. Yes, when the ugly and dead "stems" in our lives are cut off of us, they can and sometimes do hurt, but we need to remember that he does so with the intention of that pruning yielding vibrant life in its place.

FINITE OBSTACLES

Bad habits, Personal vices, Anything preventing a person from a relationship with Christ

INFINITE TRUTH

God loves us and has good plans in mind for us. We need to trust that the work he does in our lives, whether pleasant or painful, are done with an infinite and perfect plan in mind.

---

45 Cf. Matthew 6:26-34
46 Cf. Genesis 1:27
47 Cf. John 10:11
48 https://www.biblegateway.com/passage/?search=Matthew%207%3A7-12&version=NIV

PRAYER

Heavenly father, thank you for your care and good heart. Thank you for your perfect intentions and husbandry of your creation. Please forgive us of getting in the way of your plans, and help us to trust you more, knowing that you have plans to give us hope and a new life in Christ. In Jesus' holy name, amen.

LESSON 4

FORGET WHAT YOU'VE BEEN REMEMBERING

> "and said to them, 'Go over before the ark of the LORD your God into the middle of the Jordan. Each of you is to take up a stone *on his shoulder, according to the number of the tribes of the Israelites,* to serve as a sign among you. In the future, when your children ask you, 'What do these stones mean?' tell them *that the flow of the Jordan was cut off before the ark of the covenant of the LORD. When it crossed the Jordan, the waters of the Jordan were cut off. These stones are to be a memorial to the people of Israel forever'* (Emphasis the author's)."
>
> JOSHUA 4:5-7

The context of this passage is when Joshua was being led by the Lord to bring the Israelites into their promised land. They had to cross the Jordan River in order to get there, and in one of the frequently forgotten miracles of God that was no less amazing than the parting of the Red Sea, God completely stopped the flow of the Jordan River during its flood stage so that all of the Israelites could cross it on dry land. Once the people all crossed the Jordan River, God told Joshua to "...take up twelve stones (and) put them down at the place where they stay(ed) the night."[49] In following the Lord's will, Joshua told his people to take up the stones and establish an altar. Joshua then gave the reason why God commands us to set up permanent markers in our lives as well: to remember that it is God who blesses us and establishes the good in our lives, and further, so that we can teach our children and posterity the same.

The more I write the more I realize that God allowed me to experience my divorce and loss of my son, Braeden so that I could have a ministry of teaching forgiveness, overcoming bitterness, and to create a heart in me that has a passion to teach others based on my experiences. It certainly was not what I had in mind when I used to think about how I could best serve the Lord, but I want to do his will, and it is becoming increasingly apparent that speaking truth and forgiveness is my ministry. The Lord's message in the Word to Joshua was clear, and it should still be clear today. **We need to remember what we have forgotten, and we need to forget what we've been remembering.** Once again, we need to remember what we have forgotten, and we need to forget what we've been remembering.

What does this mean? If we all think back on our past, we should be able to see the handiwork of God in our lives. Some of us were abused as children by our parents or another, yet God delivered us out of that treachery. Some of us can recall an accident where we should have died or been maimed, but God's gracious hand prevented our injury. Some of us should not have been able to conceive a child, yet the Lord miraculously delivered a baby. Think back on your life and *remember* what God has done for you. Have you forgotten it? Have you taken it for granted? Have you established a permanent marker in your life as God has commanded so that when your children get older and

---

[49] Joshua 4:2-3; https://www.biblegateway.com/passage/?search=Joshua+4%3A2-3&version=NCV

ask about it, you will then have the opportunity to tell them about the Lord's graciousness in your life?

Deuteronomy 8:11-14 warns us not to forget what the Lord has done, because when we do, we have a tendency to become proud. It declares:

>>><<<

"Be careful that you do not forget the Lord your God, failing to observe his commands, his laws and his decrees that I am giving you this day. Otherwise, when you eat and are satisfied, when you build fine houses and settle down, and when your herds and flocks grow large and your silver and gold increase and all you have is multiplied, then your heart will become proud and you will forget the Lord your God, who brought you out of Egypt, out of the land of slavery."

>>><<<

Additionally, Deuteronomy 8:18 tells us to "remember the Lord your God, for it is he who gives you the ability to produce wealth, and so confirms his covenant which he swore to your forefathers, as it is today." Curiously, the last four words of this passage tell us that this command is no different today than it was when Deuteronomy was written (ca. 1400 B.C.). This is a testament on its own that God himself doesn't forget the past either.

God has called Christians to forgiveness. Jesus forgave those crucifying him even while he was hanging on the cross,[50] yet I, for two and a half years, struggled to forgive my ex-wife. I was wrong and in my own prison of guilt and bitterness. I should have forgotten what I was remembering (a re-living of the pain) and instead I should have remembered what I was forgetting (that the Lord delivered me). I was actually sinning by failing to remember God's work while at the same time sinning by failing to forgive. Now how stupid was that? God delivered me from trouble, and instead of honoring the Lord, I chose to be proud and dishonor the very one who delivered me.

America is currently under attack from some people who attempt to paint America in a negative light. While any nation made up of flawed human beings will err, our nation *has* been blessed mightily by God. It unfortunately seems that some people have forgotten the good things America has done, and as a result, many have collectively become proud. Some believe that we have

---

50   Luke 23:34; https://biblehub.com/luke/23-34.htm

established our worth, which totally goes against scripture.[51] It was God who established this nation back in 1776,[52] and the Founders made sure to give him credit in the *Declaration of Independence*. Additional study of the writings and statements of our Founding Fathers will also support the position that many believed this was one nation under God.[53] It is beyond reason to think that a fledgling group of English colonists could have defeated the world's super-power of the time without an act of God. It was the Lord who also gave us an isolated continent that remained predominantly free from foreign attacks due to the vast Atlantic and Pacific oceans. It was God who enabled us to become the global economic and military super-power that we once were, and it is God who still blesses our nation to this very day despite both our admitted and unspoken flaws. All people are but sinners created from the dust of the earth, but we are loved by God and created in his image and that is what makes us different from even the angels in heaven. These are all facts that many seem to have forgotten that should be remembered, and much of what is currently being remembered needs to quickly be forgotten.

Let us take time out today to remember some of the blessings that God has bestowed upon each and every one of us. Take just five minutes of time away from whatever you are doing to *remember* and thank the Lord for his good deeds. Ask the Lord to show you how you can establish a permanent "altar" on the banks of your own "Jordan River" so that when your children and others see it they will ask you its meaning. This will provide you an opportunity to share God's blessings and love with those people, you will be acting in obedience to God by remembering his works, and who knows...the Lord may use you and your "altar" to bring another soul into the kingdom of God.

---

51 Cf. I John 2:20 & 27; Romans 16:25; II Corinthians 5:5
52 Cf. Deuteronomy 32:8; Job 12:23; Acts 17:26
53 I would argue the most exhaustive record of American quotations that support this idea is William J. Federer's book *America's God and Country: Encyclopedia of Quotations*; Amerisearch, 2000.

FINITE OBSTACLES

Ingratitude, Selective memory, Failing to acknowledge God's hand in our lives, Self-aggrandizing pride

INFINITE TRUTH

God is worthy of our praise regardless of our circumstance, and we need to acknowledge his glory in our lives so that the honor we give him can be used to teach posterity of his worthiness.

Prayer

Dear Lord, please forgive us for forgetting you and becoming proud. Please strike the sin from our hearts that keeps us from forgiving those who have hurt us and replace it with the spirit of forgiveness. Teach us to remember you and your almighty works, and prevent us from dishonoring you through amnesia and an unforgiving mindset. Please bless our recommitment to you, and use us for your will. In the name of Jesus, amen.

Lesson 5

There Are Seven Sage Sirens

"Some people are wicked and no good. They go around telling lies, winking with their eyes, tapping with their feet, and making signs with their fingers. They make evil plans in their hearts and are always starting arguments. So trouble will strike them in an instant; suddenly they will be so hurt no one can help them. There are six things the Lord hates. There are seven things he cannot stand: a proud look, a lying tongue, hands that kill innocent people, a mind that thinks up evil plans, feet that are quick to do evil, a witness who lies, and someone who starts arguments among families."

PROVERBS 6:12-19

Ever since I was a young high school-aged child, I have always been drawn to the wisdom contained in the book of Proverbs. I can remember reading this book of the Bible more than any other over the years. In fact, I can vividly recall a time while growing up where I asked the Lord to give me wisdom over and above anything else in life. The sinful part of me wishes I had requested money rather than wisdom, but the spiritual part of me knows that I asked for and have received the better of the two requests.[54] God has answered that prayer many times, but I freely admit that it has not been of my own doing. God himself has granted me his wisdom in many areas of life, and rightfully deserves my praise and the credit for doing so. I also will add to this that some of the trials that produced that wisdom were not very easy.

In Proverbs chapter six, the Lord begins with warnings against foolishness, laziness, putting up security for another person's loan, and actions that yield poverty. Once the reader arrives at verse twelve, the Lord poignantly indicates that some people have become so corrupted by sin that they are utterly "wicked and no good." On the surface this appears counter-biblical, for we Christians believe all people can be redeemed by the blood of Christ. While this is always true - Christ's sacrifice is certainly sufficient enough to redeem anyone - people do not always receive that gracious gift. Some, as the text indicates, willfully, foolishly, and to their and other people's detriment remain in their sins to the point of pure corruption. Verse fourteen states that they "make evil plans in their hearts and are always starting arguments (i.e. are contentious)."

This information is both startling yet revealing at the same time. Since this chapter is a compilation of warnings against foolishness, it implies that failing to grasp the fact that some people are so utterly corrupt is a fool's errand. This begs the question, "With so much wickedness present in the earth, why would someone have trouble acknowledging particular people, even some who are close to us, are evil?" I think the answer to this question can be summarized in one word: Projection. We human beings tend to project our thought patterns onto others. What this means is we tend to believe that others think and act in similar ways that we think and act, but God's Word informs us that this isn't necessarily true. In fact, we deceive ourselves when we project onto others because we fail to take into consideration the depth of wickedness that an individual's own sin-nature can take a person. Some people have had enough of the Lord's influence within their lives that they generally seek good will,

---

54 cf. I Kings 3:1-15

but God also informs us that some people who have consistently rejected the Lord's influence have enabled sin to penetrate even their thoughts and plans to the point of total corruptibility.[55] This is disturbing to consider, but God shares this information with us to help keep us safe and wise.

As this chapter continues, we see that verses sixteen through nineteen is a list of indicators that act as loud sirens to help guide the wise person into recognizing behaviors that reveal when a person has become "wicked and no good." We are wise to keep these "seven things God cannot stand (tolerate)" in mind. Notice the first indicator is pride. Pride is a spirit of self-sufficiency, and any honest person will recognize that we humans are *not* self-sufficient, even those who are financially blessed. Money cannot buy the very breath of life that comes only from the Holy Spirit, nor can it buy salvation, wisdom, or joy. Those things only come from the Lord, and those things only bring peace.[56]

The second indicator that we should look out for is a lying tongue. God is the author of all truth,[57] and Satan is labeled the Father of lies.[58] "Fathers" have offspring, and a person who habitually lies to the point where deception becomes a character trait is identified as a child of Satan. Generally speaking, when we see a warning against lying people, we may automatically think of a particular person who openly lies to us. However, a lying person doesn't always lie to our faces. They can - and often do - lie to themselves, and that still makes them a liar and worthy of our caution. Take for example a person who lies to their own self by declaring there is no God. They have convinced themselves of a lie, the Bible describes this as foolish,[59] and as a result of foolishly lying to themselves, they errantly transmit that lie to others.[60] They are essentially deluded and perpetuate those delusions toward anyone who will listen. This is a person we should at the very least be cautious around. If they don't have the discipline to protect their own minds from lies, how can we be sure they won't deceive us whether it be intentional or not?

A third warning siren involves "hands that kill innocent people." At first, this one appears very straightforward. God doesn't like murderers and advises us to evade such people. While this is certainly true, there is more to "killing innocent people" than just shedding blood (murder). "Killing" can also be

---

55 Cf. II Peter 2:10-15
56 Cf. Psalm 4:8; Romans 15:13; Galatians 5:22; James 3:17; and Philippians 4:9
57 Cf. John. 17:17; Titus 1:2; Numbers 23:19
58 Cf. John 8:44 and Genesis 3:4
59 Psalm 14:1; https://biblehub.com/psalms/14-1.htm
60 https://www.biblegateway.com/passage/?search=1%20John%204:1-6&version=NIV

metaphor for any behavior that yields the death of something. Have you heard of someone "killing a party"? Marriages can also be killed. Friendships can be killed. Trust can be killed, and many other aspects of life can be "killed" too. A person who willingly takes part in "killing" something innocent is partaking in behaviors that the Lord hates. We too should hate these behaviors and pray for people who put such behaviors into continual practice. This means we should avoid a person who speaks words that would kill our marriages. People who practice behaviors that would kill our friendships probably aren't worthy of friendship in the first place. Those who betray and ultimately "kill" our trust are perhaps examples of "wicked and no good" people mentioned in verse twelve.

The fourth warning is against "a mind that thinks up evil plans." This is a person who is actively listening to his/her own sin-nature or to Satanic influences, for pure evil does just that - thinks up evil plans. People who are actively seeking wrong behaviors fall into this category. Do you know someone who "plans" their time in a manner where they constantly live in a state of corrupted behavior? Do you know someone who works in the shadows to engage in licentious behaviors out of sight? Do you recognize a person in your life who consistently endeavors bad over good? These are examples of people engaging in behaviors that God detests, and we are wise to stay away from them.

Warning five is against "feet that are quick to do evil." This is a person who has allowed Satan to so corrupt their will that they have suppressed their consciences to the point where they no longer consider what is right or wrong. They simply run toward what "feels good." They run their lives with their emotions rather than by the Word of God. English occultist Aleister Crowley captured this idea of throwing caution to the wind and doing what feels good in the phrase "Do what thou wilt shall be the whole of the law."[61]

Number six is a reiteration of number two, so we now have assurance that God really, really hates lying. A "witness who lies" is a person who circumvents truth for personal gain. A witness is called to testify on behalf of the truth, but this type of person literally contravenes the very reason they are called. This indicates corruption at an extremely deep level, and a person willing to lie for personal gain is a person for whom we need to pray.

---

[61] https://www.horuscentre.org/library/Thelema/Magick_In_Theory_And_Practice.pdf

Lastly, the seventh warning is against "someone who starts arguments among families." This is a person with little to no regard for what God has created and ordained. God created the family in the Garden of Eden. God is a God of relationships, and family is the first and tightest relationship for most people. A person who works against relationships is a person working on behalf of Satan. He wants nothing more than to destroy families, so a person who sows enough discord to start arguments within families is working against God's will. Adulterers are especially good at starting family quarrels. Hateful people fall into this category as well. Let choose not to be quarrelers and instead be diligent to bring life to our families by sowing seeds of love, honor, respect, and benevolence.

Thankfully, God did not leave his creation in the dark when it comes to identifying bad influences. This list of seven loud warning sirens should be studied so that when we recognize them, we can be cognizant of potential negative influences in our lives. It is a pleasure to know that we serve a God who loves us enough to give us indicators of behaviors that reveal deeply corrupt thinking, but it is likewise a source of information we should also use to help guide our prayers. God loves every person and wants all people to come to salvation.[62] When we are able to identify these traits in a person, we are wise to steer clear of their influence but we should still pray that the Lord convicts them unto repentance. We have to always remember, we too were once lost and it is only by the grace of God that we were rescued from such behaviors.

FINITE OBSTACLES

Humanity's tendency to project their own thought processes onto others despite evidence that may contradict what we are projecting.

INFINITE TRUTH

Evil is real, and although the father of evil is invisible to the natural eye, his visible children do produce fruit we can observe to help us make wise decisions around them. We therefore need to remain cognizant of the fruit produced in people's lives.

---

62 Cf. I Timothy 2:4; II Peter 3:9

PRAYER

Lord, give us the wisdom to recognize people who are working against your Kingdom rather than for it. We are not allowed to despise these people but we are warned to avoid them, so I ask that you give us the ability to discern between Kingdom-workers and Kingdom-assailants. I also pray that your spirit enlightens them to a point where they confess their sins and repent. You are not willing that any should perish, but as a righteous God, we know you will righteously allow sin to receive its just due, and that is a terrible truth for those who reject your Son. In Christ's name, amen.

Lesson 6

God's Omniscience Isn't A License To Avoid Prayer

"Do not be anxious about anything, but in every situation, by prayer and petition, with thanksgiving, present your requests to God."

Philippians 4:6

A question was recently posed to me that goes as follows: "If God is omniscient (all-knowing), then what's the point of praying? After all, isn't God going to do what he wants to?"

After considering this question in the moment, a few ideas popped into my mind, but I could not in my opinion solidly answer the question. After that dialogue concluded, I later began to search for a good answer since I was dissatisfied with my ignorance. Rather than seeking an answer from the Lord, I first attempted to "Google" the question, and when I would come to a link and read it, I felt the Lord pressuring me within my heart saying, "Rob, why don't you ask me instead of Google?" After ignoring that urging for a few minutes (like a fool) and not finding a fulfilling answer, I eventually did ask the Lord for guidance in prayer and began to search his Word for a plausible answer.

The first thing that came to my mind relates to the "asking Google instead of God" situation stated in the paragraph above. If praying to God really doesn't make a difference as my friend's question implied, then why does God impress upon us the idea that we should consult him for certain answers rather than an internet search engine?[63] God obviously seeks our interaction with him, and he apparently sought to assist me with my ignorance.[64] Jesus thought so highly of prayer that in Matthew 6:9-13, he actually took the time to model how we should pray. This passage has come to be known as the Lord's Prayer, and recorded are the actual words of Jesus himself. Jesus declares in verse nine, "This, then, is how you should pray:" How great is it that God-incarnate taught his followers that we should pray, and then goes on to offer a sample guideline by which we can follow? If Jesus himself taught us to pray, the first lesson to learn is just that...we *should* pray because God encourages us to do so and even modeled it for us. God already knows that he knows everything ahead of time, yet he still tells us to pray.

Secondly, by God encouraging us to pray to him, this reveals his desire that we be in a relationship with him.[65] We also discover that the Lord instructs us to pray so that the Father may rightfully be glorified.[66] God could easily "miracle" wisdom into our minds without us asking, but by doing it that way, God knows we would miss out on the growth experiences that come through prayer and waiting for an answer. Furthermore, if he were not interested in our prayers because of his omniscience, he would not be including us in his plans, and that is out of character for God.[67] He loves us so much that he seeks to have a relationship with us, and by our act of praying to God, this is a means of establishing and strengthening that relationship. This is why Christianity is different from all other religions. It is actually not a religion; it is a relationship with the almighty Creator.

---

[63] Cf. James 1:5
[64] Cf. Matthew 7:9-11
[65] Cf. Matthew 11:28-29; Proverbs 3:5-6; Romans 5:8; John 3:16
[66] John 14:13; https://www.biblehub.com/john/14-13.htm. For more scriptural support of prayer rightfully glorifying God, see Isaiah 66:18-19; Psalm 96:4-9, 86:12; II Corinthians 4:13-15.
[67] Cf. Ephesians 2:10; John 15:1-27; Ephesians 3:20

Thirdly, by praying, we also get to witness the effects of our prayers. Matthew 18:19-20 informs us that we interact with and rely on the Holy Spirit when we pray. Luke 1:13 shows us that God hears our prayer requests and sometimes grants them. Luke 6:12 shows us that even Jesus went before God in prayer before making important decisions. He prayed all night before selecting (even though he already knew beforehand) who his twelve disciples would be. We even see the disciples remaining "in constant prayer" before making the important decision of selecting a replacement for the betrayer, Judas Iscariot, in Acts 1:12-14. I Timothy 1-4 is a group of passages where Paul urges Christians to pray, intercede, and give thanks for everyone. It also informs us that doing so is "good and pleases God..." There are many, many other passages that discuss prayer in the Bible (eighty-eight passages by my count), but I still cannot find a verse that specifically tells us the answer to our initially proposed question.

So what do we do then? I think Isaiah chapter fifty-five holds some of the answers to this mystery. Verses eight through eleven are the famous, "My thoughts are not your thoughts, and my ways are not your ways..." verses. There are simply some things God has not elected to fully disclose to us, but we can be assured God is in total and complete control. He even references the water cycle in these passages as an example of something not totally understood by man, but since he created it, he knows the intricate details of it. He also declares in verse eleven that the words that proceed out of his mouth, "will not return to (him) empty but accomplish what (he) desires and achieve the purpose for which (he) sent it." Application of this is as follows: God tells us to pray. He gives us many examples in the Bible – both Old and New Testaments – of people who pray and do so for some certain reasons. Jesus himself prayed and encouraged us to do so. These stories are all part of God's Word, which he declares accomplishes his purposes. We may not know those purposes he seeks to accomplish, but it is clear he wants to include us in fulfilling them. That is sometimes done through prayer.

In sum, there are questions we may have, the answers of which God chooses not to reveal sometimes (such as the time and hour of Christ's return). We do know, however, that he is omniscient and certainly does not need us to do as he pleases. Yet he still gave us eighty-eight separate passages of man praying to him for various reasons. Some prayers are left unanswered like Paul's request to remove his thorn, and some, even many, are answered. God loves us enough to include us in his will even though he does not need any of our contributions. And one last thing...Genesis 18:20-33 and II Kings 19:1-7 are two examples of how the prayer of men actually influenced God's divine will. Did God know his will would be affected? Of course, but he also intended to do something else and provided men the opportunity to allow him to show his grace instead of his righteous judgment. God lovingly showed compassion on mankind; mankind's relationship with God was strengthened; mankind learned the power of prayer; and God was glorified because of the process.

We may not always know why we should pray or if our prayers will be answered, but we do know God will hear them and will include us in his will somehow if we are one of his children.[68] This is why his thoughts and ways are far above our ways. He is God; we are simply followers who are entrusted with grace to do his will, and part of that means we trust him enough to pray to him.

FINITE OBSTACLES
Doubt, Ignorance, Skepticism

INFINITE TRUTH
God is omniscient and omnipotent, but he truly desires mankind to be engaged in a relationship with him. In order for this relationship to occur, God offered his own son as a sacrifice so that we can enter that relationship through grace.

---

[68] Cf. I John 3:22

PRAYER

Lord, teach us to pray. Please allow us to learn through prayer, and be glorified by our prayers. In Jesus' name, amen.

Lesson 7

> "Oh, the depth of the riches of the wisdom and knowledge of God! How unsearchable his judgments, and his paths beyond tracing out! 'Who has known the mind of the Lord? Or who has been his counselor'?"
>
> ROMANS 11:33-34

When I was a child, I was able to play just about any sport that was available to me. I would race anyone who would run a race against me. I rode my bike everywhere. I played football, baseball, hockey, basketball, and racquetball. As I got old enough to be more self-aware, I realized that the Lord had made me an athlete, and I tended to do well in anything I tried. This gift ended up being a coin with two sides, however. On the one hand, I experienced lots of fun and success when I was involved in sports. On the other hand, the success I witnessed served to build up my pride to the point where I had an unhealthy confidence in anything I did. Even as a young adult, I was very successful. My body was simply gifted to do things that many others could not. However, at the age of forty-five, I had a mini-stroke, which ultimately led to doctors discovering that I had cancer. After going through the surgeries and undergoing radiation treatments, what was once an active and powerful body succumbed to the cruel after-effects of these tiny, invisible particles that bombarded my body. The radiation had zapped me of so much vitality that I could barely manage to walk up one flight of stairs. Even today, some three years later, my once-strong legs sometimes shake as I go down a flight of stairs. What were once vigorous legs of strength and agility turned into legs that often feel like dry, hardened clay.

If I were to attempt athletic activity now, I very likely would crumble underneath the stress of the exertion. What now feel like dry, brittle legs could never run in a manner they once did. Just as my bodily foundation has broken down, many of us experience moments in our lives that serve to attack our mental foundation as well. Cancer also has a way of testing one's mental and emotional resilience, and as I go through this process, I am pressed to depend on God's supernatural strength to survive some of the days. I am grateful, however, that this physical challenge has opened my eyes to the truth that despite the attacks that come our way, God never has jettisoned me despite my condition. I am living proof that our strength can be renewed and we can "run" the race of life without growing weary if our hope is rightfully placed in the Lord Jesus.[69]

There was a time earlier in my life when I depended upon my own strength to combat life's daily struggles, and in those days, I often failed miserably. That is not to say that I still do not fail, but I certainly have learned one of God's infinite mysteries, and that is to depend upon God for strength even during the times when it feels like he is not around. This is often challenging but a "must" if I am to honor God's Word. This is also detrimental to making it through this very tough world with a positive attitude.

The apostle Paul speaks of this concept in our focal verses. After contemplating how Israel will one day be saved and writing some of the revealed mystery of this salvation, Paul finishes his letter to the Roman Christians with

---

[69] Isaiah 40:31; https://www.biblehub.com/isaiah/40-31.htm

a doxology. He begins his comment with the word "Oh," as if he is looking down a deep cavern and amazed by its seeming infinitude. Paul tells us that the mind of God is infinite. His wisdom, his plans, the answers to all of the "Whys?" that have been asked throughout the millennia are captured with these two verses. God's knowledge of why he allows some things to happen in life are part of the riches that belong only to him. God's ability to know the right answer for every question in life and beyond are part of his wisdom and glory.[70] His ways are unfathomable by finite mankind. This is why Paul could rhetorically declare, "Who has known the mind of the Lord?"

So how does this information help us during our struggles in life? The answer to this has required much prayer, study of God's Word, and consistent seeking of wisdom from God. I posit that being able to grasp this lesson (as imperfectly as I have been able to grasp it) requires a modicum of spiritual maturity. That may sound a bit conceited and before I am labeled this way, I want to declare that only by God sharing a tidbit of his wisdom with me have I been able to taste but a drop of this lesson. Deuteronomy 29:29 declares, "The secret things belong to the LORD our God, but the things revealed belong to us and to our children forever, that we may follow all the words of this law." God does reveal tidbits of his mysteries – his "secret things" – so that we may continue our walk with him. However, he does so only if we ask. James 1:5 tells us that if we lack wisdom, we should ask, and God will give us wisdom. He does not promise us that he will reveal everything, though. Job found this out when he underwent his terrible trials. Even though the three friends who gave him counsel did not give him the best of advice at times, Job's friend Zophar was wise enough to remind Job that God's mysteries cannot be fathomed by man.[71] Job was later able to make it through all of his travails because he maintained faith and trusted God's providence alone.

Now let me attempt to tie all of this difficult lesson together. Life is absolutely hard regardless of the situations in which we find ourselves. The wealthy often have difficulty with self-aggrandizement and the ever-deceptive temptation of pride. The impoverished often struggle with self-pity. Some people face bigoted persecution due to a certain belief or practice, while others

---

[70] Cf. Deuteronomy 29:29; Proverbs 25:2
[71] Job 11:7-9; https://www.biblegateway.com/passage/?search=job%2011:7-9&version=NIV

have to face the fact that they are one of the bigoted persecutors of others made in the image of God. All Christians particularly remain under an unceasing declaration of war by our enemy, Satan. Regardless of your particular temptations and received attacks, a maturing Christian can find peace and rest even during times of uncertainty. God is sovereign. God knows "mysteries," some of which we will never know. I may never find out the entirety of why God allowed me to lose my son. I may never learn the mystery of why I and many others have had cancer. I may never know why the Lord allowed my and Renee's two children to perish before we were able to know them. There are many, many other mysteries in life that I will perhaps never know until glory, but I am able to find comfort and peace even in these circumstances because I know God is sovereign.[72]

Because God has brought me to a point in my spiritual walk where I have been humbled enough to know that it is sometimes not my business to know everything, I can be at peace with a lack of answers. In fact, many of the times I demanded answers, seeking to know more than I was allowed to know were prideful and sinful times. I, in effect, attempted to place myself on an even plane with God who does indeed know everything. This was idolatry, with me attempting to be God. There is nothing wrong with asking God for wisdom to make it through situations in life, but when we feel we *have* to know everything, we tend to sin as well as try to accomplish the impossible. We essentially bang our heads against an idolatrous wall. The depth of God's wisdom is impossible for us to attain. This is why Paul began his doxology with an emphatic "Oh." I would argue that word should have been followed with multiple exclamation points. It could read, "Oh!!!! The depth of God's wisdom..." I had this same kind of thought when I first looked down at the depth of the Grand Canyon in Arizona. Without trying to sound blasphemous, I remember thinking "Oh!!!! That thing is deep!" in a similar manner.

God knows why he allows events to occur in our lives that we would never let occur if we had an option. Romans 8:28 informs us that God will take "all things" (both good and bad) and make them work for our good. Resting in the peace of faith in God's omniscience can be one of the most soothing remedies for life's difficult endeavors. Accepting the fact that we may never find out why

---

[72] Cf. Jeremiah 32:17; Isaiah 25:8-9; Psalm 115:3; Colossians 1:16; Matthew 19:26

bad things happen to us brings about a mature spiritual walk that God desires for us. Life is extremely hard, and it is much harder for some than others, but we have to remind ourselves that God will strengthen us each day so that we can make it to our final destination of heaven. Once we get there, we have all of eternity to pick God's brain for why things happened the way they did. Have faith in our righteous and loving God, and it will deliver to you a strength that will allow you to soar on wings of eagles.[73]

FINITE OBSTACLES

Self-aggrandizement, Thinking we must know all of the answers to life, Physical bodies that wear down with age and disease

INFINITE TRUTH

Despite our frailties and sin nature, if we are in Christ, we have an unlimited amount of strength and wisdom from which we can draw.

---

73 Cf. Isaiah 40:31

Prayer

Heavenly father, I thank you for the opportunity to pray to a God who loves us and wants to hear from us. Thank you for informing us that we can tap into your infinite strength and gain wisdom simply by asking. I ask that you help us to depend on you more, especially in times when we are under attack. Please help us to remain faithful to you even when you are silent. May we find rest from our burdens in Jesus. In Christ's name, amen.

LESSON 8

"The words of Amos, one of the shepherds of Tekoa – what he saw concerning Israel two years before the earthquake, when Uzziah was king of Judah and Jereboam son of Jehoash was king of Israel" (emphasis the author's).

AMOS 1:1

Since Amos has gone down in history as a Biblically-recorded prophet, it is clear that he was a man called by God to deliver a message for God. Whenever you hear the identifying statement, "He is a man of God," what comes to mind? Do you think of an historical figure such as Moses? Perhaps you consider a more contemporary person such as Billy Graham? Maybe you think a man of God is the pastor of your church. Whether the person you consider is an heir to the Egyptian throne, a simple man from the

United States, or a local pastor who may have a wall of scholarly diplomas, or a man working for a church part-time, a focus on a "man of God's" worldly status is unwise. Amos by trade was simply that of a lowly shepherd, but his obedience to his calling is what made him an influencer for the Lord. While herding sheep appears an insignificant job to most, an evaluation of Amos' effectiveness for the Kingdom does not reflect what he was called to do vocationally. It is easy for us to admire what the world considers a successful person, but it is much harder for us to honor the nondescript person labeled by the world as unimportant or meaningless. Such a myopic view is not helpful to our spiritual walk, and I have to admit that I have been guilty of judging my usefulness to God with this dangerous nearsightedness. I have called into question whether or not I am making a difference for God's Kingdom by inappropriately focusing on my profession. This may sound silly to some, as I am an educator, but the temptation to insert the words "just a" in front of my profession sometimes occurs. This causes me to lose sight of who really is important in the first place. True influence never really comes from us, for we are simply the "vessels for honorable use,"[74] as "temples of the Holy Spirit."[75] The power of our influence comes from God, not us.[76] The real truth is the fact that all of us are "just a __," and recognition of this enables us to serve God from the appropriate position of humility. Once we accept this fact, it is then that we can best be used of God.

Perhaps at some point in his life, Amos may also have questioned his own impact for God, thinking he was just one of many "shepherds from Tekoa." Perhaps you too have desired to make an impact for the kingdom but also fell for the lie that you can't be effective due to an unremarkable status. I know I sometimes struggle at times with believing that I make an impact in the world as a common educator since I can impact only a small group in this huge world of billions of people. Those times when I question how much impact I am having, I have to remind myself that I am doing vital work for the Lord's kingdom because I am attempting to follow his will for my life. Amos too followed God's will for his life by tending sheep, and that did not stop the Lord from using him. I once heard the late pastor Adrian Rogers say, "You may be too big for God to use you, but you'll never be too small." There are times in

---

[74] II Timothy 2:21; https://biblehub.com/2_timothy/2-21.htm
[75] I Corinthians 6:19-20; https://www.biblegateway.com/passage/?search=1+Corinthians+6%3A19-20&version=ESV
[76] Cf. II Corinthians 4:7

my life when I have to repeat those sage words to myself when I feel useless. They help me refocus on the fact that it is not me who makes a difference anyway; it is Christ who makes the difference through me. I am simply the vessel. Just like any other person with a sane mind, I also want to know that what I do has meaning, but we have to accept the fact that our meaningfulness is not of our own works. It is instead by the grace of God that we are able to bear fruit for his kingdom.[77]

Amos was simply a sheep-herding, average man, but he allowed God to guide him and direct him even though to the world he was nobody special. We must understand that we too are ordinary people who serve an extraordinary God. God works his will *through* the lives of obedient people regardless of what the world may declare about their position. We need to daily be in his Word so that we can discern his will for our lives, and as we live that life and remain in close communion with our heavenly Father, it is then that we will see meaning. I want to encourage you today with the idea that just as he did in Amos' life, God can also work extraordinary and vital things through our lives regardless of our occupation or status in life. It is not the job or privilege that makes the difference. It is God who makes the difference in our lives. Never allow your position in life to allow you to become complacent in the kingdom. We know that doing things for the kingdom will bear fruit if we do not give up.[78]

FINITE OBSTACLES

Worldly status, A misunderstanding of how great God truly is, A misunderstanding of how lowly mankind is due to his sin nature

INFINITE TRUTH

"For from him, through him, and to him are all things,"[79] and this includes our value and contributions to the Kingdom.

---

77 Cf. John 15:1-8
78 Cf. Galatians 6:9
79 Romans 11:36; https://www.biblehub.com/romans/11-36.htm

PRAYER

Heavenly Father, thank you for your love and guidance in life. Thank you that you are truly the difference-maker in the world. Thank you for our jobs and positions in life. Please first grant us contentment for where you currently have us in life, and then please grant us repentance for failing to fully trust your guidance and will for our lives. Please cleanse us of any thoughts or actions of resistance to your instruction, and I pray you convict us of sins we commit that block communion with you. I humble myself before you and ask you to continue to work in our lives, enabling us to allow you to use our gifts for the advancement of your kingdom. Please strengthen us in our areas of weakness, and ignite in us a spark of boldness for your sake. Forgive us of our selfish sins and remind us that we are a chosen people not because of what we do but because of the work Jesus Christ did for us and in us. I ask these things in the name of our Lord and savior, Jesus, amen.

LESSON 9

GET "UN-STUCK" IN YOUR WAYS

> This is what the LORD Almighty says: "These people say, 'The time has not yet come for the LORD's house to be built'." Then the word of the LORD came through the prophet Haggai: "Is it a time for you yourselves to be living in your paneled houses, while this house remains a ruin?" Now this is what the LORD Almighty says: "Give careful thought to your ways. You have planted much, but have harvested little. You eat, but never have enough. You drink, but never have your fill. You put on clothes, but are not warm. You earn wages, only to put them in a purse with holes in it." This is what the LORD Almighty says: "Give careful thought to your ways. Go up into the mountains and bring down timber and build the house, so that I may take pleasure in it and be honored," says the LORD. "You expected much,

> *but see, it turned out to be little. What you brought home, I blew away. Why?" declares the LORD Almighty. "Because of my house, which remains a ruin, while each of you is busy with his own house. Therefore, because of you the heavens have withheld their dew and the earth its crops. I called for a drought on the fields and the mountains, on the grain, the new wine, the oil and whatever the ground produces, on men and cattle, and on the labor of your hands."*
>
> HAGGAI 1:2-11

Think back to a time when you watched a person do or say something that you personally disagreed with or did not like. For me, I get frustrated the way some people drive. Others may be bothered by the way their spouses do or don't do some household chores, while others may be bothered the way someone communicates with them. We've all heard the cliché statement, "He's stuck in his ways," and we understand this to mean that the person we speak of has a way of doing things that aren't going to change regardless of our response to their actions. When we declare the aforementioned statement, we in essence are declaring, "He's not going to change the way he does things." Well…neither will God.

One thing we sinful humans have extreme difficulty with is understanding that God too has a way that he does things, and since he is eternal, one could really argue that God is *definitely* stuck in his ways. He has been doing things his way long before you or I were even a twinkle in someone's eye. This is why the Lord lovingly tells us in Haggai 1:5 & 7 to "Give careful thought to *your* ways" (emphasis mine). Perhaps the Lord said the same thing twice to get our attention to the statement's importance. He knows we are born inherently selfish and want to do things our way, but we apparently don't seem to recognize this as well as we should. Thus, we receive the double reminder. As we read further, we also discover that God will sometimes intentionally thwart our efforts when they are done "our way" so that we get so frustrated that we give up "our way" and preferably adopt God's way. Since God is perfect, who would be the better one to emulate: our way or a perfect and loving God's way?

Despite this being a rhetorical question, I observe in myself and often times in those around me that we still usually try to do things our way, and when God does frustrate our endeavors, our response is not to give up our plans but to dig our heels in and work at them even harder. This only yields even more frustration, and if we fail to "give careful thought to our ways," many times physical and spiritual decay sets in.

How do these two forms of decay begin to affect us? If we continue on our own path and neglect God's truths, this is when we first begin to experience failures. They may be small at first, but we progressively become aware of our own futility. This should drive us toward God. If it does not, I know I have tended to delve deeper into the depths of selfishness and experienced even more failure, and perhaps you have too. While we should be angry with our own stubbornness, we instead tend to get mad at God. This spiritual assault from within ourselves then begins to manifest itself without, and our internal anger often spills out of us in the form of external bitterness. When bitterness begins corrupting our family and work lives, we usually find ourselves driving others away from us. Even worse, the saddest manifestation of bitterness is that our own physical well-being and safety is eventually attacked by the internal vitriol we harbor. If we fail to daily evaluate ourselves as God twice tells us to do, we place ourselves in a position of vulnerability to be assaulted by Satan. He seeks to destroy us, and when we try to live life our way, selfishly focus on what we want, and build our own lives instead of letting God build our lives through us, we set ourselves up for defeat and much frustration.

We read in Haggai 1:5 that the children of God "planted much but harvested little." They "drank but never had their fill." They worked hard and earned money, but it always disappeared because it was placed in "purses with a large holes" in them. Ask yourself after reviewing these scriptures: Who produces a harvest? Who enables us to feel satisfaction? Who blesses our monetary earnings? And who do you think ensured their purses were full of holes? God is the one who produces, satisfies, and blesses, and he provides those gifts when we properly operate under his economy. He also makes it clear in his Word that he chastises those he loves,[80] and he purposely made sure their selfish hard work resulted in frustration because their motives were not in accordance with God's course of action. In Isaiah 55:7-9, God calls us to forsake

---

80 Cf. Psalm 3:12 and Hebrews 12:6

our ways and adopt his because his ways are so much better than ours. When we fail to do this, it reflects a rebellious heart within us. When we remain stuck in our own ways, we reflect selfishness, which tends to yield anger and then bitterness when we don't get our way. As the overflowing streams of bitterness begin to soak into other aspects of our lives, we experience frustration with our jobs, our hobbies, and our friends and families, which then manifests itself into self-induced isolation and neglect of those things which were designed by God to be of utmost importance. Eventually, if we continue to remain in our sinful ways, this can result in physical impairments such as high blood pressure, excessive stress, depression, and even physical death in some cases. This is quite a process, but I have personally experienced how bitterness can drive others away. So may have you. For what reason does God sometimes withhold his generous hand? It may be because we are not spiritually right with God. We may not be in lock-step with his ways. When this happens, we certainly are not fulfilling his will for our lives, and he loves us enough to chasten us into a position where we begin obeying his Word.

The harder we work solely for ourselves and neglect our spiritual life, the harder God works against us because that is his way of operating[81] and this doesn't even account for the nefarious actions of our enemy who is always attacking us. When we spend all of our energies trying to operate according to our plans, we have much less energy and vigor because we are ignoring the spiritual power of the Holy Spirit who lives inside us.[82] And because the Holy Spirit dwells inside us,[83] "we are no longer our own,"[84] which means we can no longer call all of the shots even though our flesh wants us to. When we try to do so, we miss out on supernatural blessings. However, when we put God first; when we change our ways to match his ways of doing things, that is when he opens up his storehouses and fulfills our lives with "good things"[85] and "with everything pertaining to life and godliness."[86] Once we make "the Lord our shepherd,"[87] it is then that we can experience true contentment with the provisions he bestows. Once we place God first in our lives and live that way, he will fulfill our deepest needs and give us the abundant life Christ

---

81   Cf. Psalm 66:7
82   Cf. I Corinthians 3:16
83   Cf. Romans 8:9
84   I Corinthians 6:19; https://biblehub.com/1_corinthians/6-19.htm
85   Proverbs 28:10; https://biblehub.com/proverbs/28-10.htm
86   II Peter 1:3; https://biblehub.com/2_peter/1-3.htm
87   Psalm 23:1; https://biblehub.com/psalms/23-1.htm

referenced.[88] If we place him anywhere but first, all of our efforts are ultimately futile. Caring for our own lives while failing to "give careful thought to our ways" and neglecting our relationship with the Lord will lead to ruin, so why don't we get "un-stuck" out of our ways and on-board with God's ways?

FINITE OBSTACLES

Selfish desires to have things "our way,"
Bitterness, Anger, Biblical ignorance

INFINITE TRUTH

God has a way he does things, and it behooves us to learn that way and fall into line with it. Once we do this, we begin experiencing the "abundant life" Christ referenced.

---

88 Cf. John 10:10

Prayer

Dear Lord, in the name of Jesus, I ask you to convict us in the deepest recesses of our hearts of our selfishness and sin. Please expose that in our lives which we cling to in hopes of need-fulfillment, and assist us with turning it over to you. Forgive us of trying to live life "our way" and help us to permanently change our ways into your ways. Turn our hearts toward you, and protect us from the onslaughts of Satan as we attempt to live the life to which you have called us. In the name of our risen Savior, Jesus Christ, amen.

LESSON 10

REMEMBER. DON'T FORGET.

"Be careful that you do not forget the LORD your God, failing to observe his commands, his laws and his decrees that I am giving you this day. Otherwise, when you eat and are satisfied, when you build fine houses and settle down, and when your herds and flocks grow large and your silver and gold increase and all you have is multiplied, then your heart will become proud and you will forget the LORD your God, who brought you out of Egypt, out of the land of slavery."

DEUTERONOMY 8:11-14

At the time I am writing this lesson, the end of January approaches and most of us will soon start receiving our W-2s for taxation purposes. As I think about taxes and whether they truly do or don't affect the American economy, I cannot help but reflect back to the year 2000. The Clinton Administration had just concluded. The American economy at the time was perceived to be extremely strong and rolling along due to the advent of public Internet business opportunities. Americans were in the midst of the SUV craze, gas was cheap, and it very much appeared that God's favorable hand was upon our nation. For me, the year 2000 brought about the highest numerical figure I had ever earned for an annual salary at that time and for many years after, and I recall feeling like I was "on top of the world" because life seemed to be going so well. Many others financially benefitted from the growth of the Internet, but by October of 2002, most of the gains people experienced from technology investments evaporated. This period of recession became known as the bursting of the "Dotcom Bubble."[89]

As I have grown wiser and better able to reflect and evaluate my life from a Godly perspective, I admit that the confident feeling I had at the turn of the 21st century was simply a false perception of affluence because I based that confidence on my own actions (my earnings). Just like the stock market gains many experienced during this time, my confidence also ended up bursting shortly thereafter because neither was rooted in the Lord. To the world (an me at the time), it appeared that I was successful. I had left the U.S. Navy debt-free just two years prior. I bought a house while at the tender age of 25. I had a wife and two beautiful children. It appeared that I was living an 'All-American' life, but that wasn't true. I also recall rarely ever thanking the Lord for the blessings he bestowed upon my family, and I do so with shame. The longer I have lived and the more people I have gotten to know deeply, the more I have discovered that my situation is not uncommon for many families.

I now realize why I failed to show the Lord much gratitude back then. It was because I was living a sinful life, and my own pride foolishly resulted in me thinking I accomplished everything on my own. After all, I was the one who got up every day and worked hard. I was the one who came up with solutions to my problems. It was always "I, I, I," or "me, me, me." I honestly believed back then that it was because of my efforts that we were able to overcome many of

---

[89] For more information, see: https://vantagepointtrading.com/trading-glossary/trading-glossary-1/2000-tech-bubble-and-stock-market-crash/

the struggles my family and I had experienced during my service time in the U.S. Navy. Now that I am able to humbly look back and review my life, it is a painful yet easy truth to admit that I was foolish. It is also clear that my loving Lord allowed me to go through a horrible time right after that low-point of extreme selfishness in order to humble me so that I might recognize the real source of any prosperity. The lesson for which I am most appreciative is that God allowed me to authentically gain an understanding of what truly satisfies[90] versus what snares[91] men and ends up as "a mouth full of gravel."[92]

The Israelites were delivered out of Egyptian slavery by God through Moses, and instead of thanking and worshipping God they grumbled and turned to worshipping a golden calf.[93] God therefore allowed the Israelites to also go through a time of troubles to eliminate the pride and foolishness from among them as well as to judge their terrible sin. They roamed the Arabian desert for forty years until all but two of the adults died.[94] Once God's chosen people were ready to be delivered into the promised land, Moses gave the above warning found in Deuteronomy chapter eight. He warned them not to forget that the Lord's hand was upon them even during their forty years of roaming the wilderness and gave examples of the fact that their clothes didn't wear out during that time and how God had miraculously fed and watered them in a desert. Furthermore, Moses knew that the Israelites would gain much material wealth once in the Promised Land, but he also understood man's sinful nature tended to cause him to forget the true source of prosperity. Knowing this, the sage instrument of deliverance warned his people not to get proud and forget that it is the Lord who blesses and who satisfies. Their ancestors who never made it out of the desert failed to acknowledge God, became proud, and were therefore destroyed as a result. I too fell under the same curse delivered by Moses in Deuteronomy 8:19.[95] What life I had then was utterly and completely destroyed between the years 2003 - 2005. However, I praise the Lord Jesus Christ for resurrecting me from that old life of depravity and pride and giving me a new life devoted to service for his kingdom. My physical life was spared, but the façade I was living was indeed destroyed.

---

90 Cf. II Corinthians 5:21 and Hebrews 10:10
91 Cf. I Timothy 6:7-10
92 Proverbs 20:17; https://biblehub.com/proverbs/20-17.htm
93 Cf. Exodus chapter 32
94 Cf. Numbers 14:30
95 https://biblehub.com/deuteronomy/8-19.htm

Thanks to this extremely hard lesson that I had to endure over multiple years, I am now able to "remember the Lord" and know that every bit of my provisions and blessings come from him. I can now openly write that I did nothing this past year that God did not enable me to do. I am satisfied with the monetary and worldly possessions with which God chooses to give to my family, but I am eternally grateful and indebted to Christ for the salvation he has granted me. It is not because I am able to do it; no, it is because the Lord blesses those who he loves![96] I am now "careful not to forget the Lord my God, who brought me out of the slavery of sin" and delivered me unto works of righteousness for his sake.[97] I don't ever want to re-learn that lesson, and my prayer is that those of you who read this will take a look at your own lives and consider just how God has blessed you.

FINITE OBSTACLES
Self-Reliance, Pride, Self-Assurance, Ingratitude

INFINITE TRUTH
All good things come from God, and it is good for us to give thanks for all of the blessings we receive whether they are great or small.

---

96 Cf. James 1:25
97 Ephesians 2:8-10; https://www.biblegateway.com/passage/?search=Ephesians%202:8-10&version=ESV

PRAYER

Lord, thank you for your loving and chastising hand that destroys sin and allows righteousness to bloom in its place. Thank you for the difficult times you brought unto me; those times that I now count as joy (James. 1:2-3) because they developed in me traits that you desired in my life. Please help us to thank you on a routine basis for the blessings and favor you have shown us, which include times of trials. We know that you are a good, loving, and gracious God, and we acknowledge that and praise you. In the holy and blessed name of Jesus, amen.

Prayer

LESSON 11

IT'S FAITH, NOT LOGIC

> "Then an angel of the Lord appeared to him, standing at the right side of the altar of incense. When Zechariah saw him, he was startled and was gripped with fear. But the angel said to him: 'Do not be afraid, Zechariah; your prayer has been heard. Your wife Elizabeth will bear you a son, and you are to give him the name John. He will be a joy and delight to you, and many will rejoice because of his birth, for he will be great in the sight of the Lord. He is never to take wine or other fermented drink, and he will be filled with the Holy Spirit even from birth. Many of the people of Israel will he bring back to the Lord their God. And he will go on before the Lord, in the spirit and power of Elijah, to turn the hearts of the fathers to their children and the disobedient

> *to the wisdom of the righteous—to make ready a people prepared for the Lord.' Zechariah asked the angel, 'How can I be sure of this? I am an old man and my wife is well along in years.' The angel answered, 'I am Gabriel. I stand in the presence of God, and I have been sent to speak to you and to tell you this good news. And now you will be silent and not able to speak until the day this happens, because you did not believe my words, which will come true at their proper time'."*
>
> LUKE 1:11-20

Luke's account of the Christmas story is one of the most often-read passages of the Bible, especially during the month of December. In their entirety, Luke chapters one and two are the most detailed of the four gospel accounts of the Christmas story. While there are certainly numerous lessons that can be learned from these two chapters, this lesson is not about Christmas. Instead, I want to center our attention on our joy, how it can be silenced, and how to prevent this from happening.

For a long time, I have felt the Lord wanting me to write and publish. One of the gifts he gave me was the ability to write, and it is my firm belief that I am to glorify and honor God with that gift. I prayed many times in the past, asking him to do what needed to be done for me to publish. However, I have to admit that while I believed he has called me to write, I doubted that anything I wrote could be published. My lack of faith very likely prevented me from realizing a long-held dream. A careful review of our verses above will reveal that I was not the first person to ever doubt God, and that actually makes me feel better despite my past failure. Even the father of a major Biblical figure struggled with doubt.

In verse eleven, we read that God sent an angel to appear to a righteous and upright priest named Zechariah. The angel comforted Zechariah's predictable initial fears, and then delivered a message from God to him. The message declared to the old man with no children was that he would one day have a son, and he was to name that son "John." Back in Biblical times, people named their children much differently than we do today. We usually pick out a name that sounds good with our last names or one that may have some sort of ties to our heritage. Biblical Jewish cultures often named children out of circumstance,[98] and the name chosen often bore significance.[99] In other words, they gave names to their children that made a statement about the circumstances surrounding the child and that held meaning for that child and his or her parents. There are only six couples listed in the Bible who were directed by God to give a specific name to their child. Zechariah's son John was one of these people whom God chose to name.[100]

According to one naming website,[101] the name John means "God is gracious." God sent an angel down with specific instructions to notify Zechariah that his and his wife's prayers had been heard by God, to foretell Zechariah of a coming son, and to instruct him that he was to give him the explicit name of "God is gracious." The fact that God was sure to name this child "John" indicated that God's grace was upon Zechariah's house. Furthermore, John would be a (v. 14) joy and delight to his family, yet Zechariah's response to God's grace was disbelief, a lack of acknowledging it, and an absence of faith. How did this angel respond to Zechariah's ill-advised yet common response? With another message from God.

The angel first identified himself as Gabriel. Out of the multitude of innumerable angels, only five are named in the Bible. Gabriel is one, and he is no ordinary, run-of-the-mill angel. In fact, he "stands in the presence of God."[102] Therefore, the words he delivers were very likely heard by Gabriel right out of God's mouth in his very throne room. Simply put, Gabriel does not spread hearsay. He actually repeats the literal words of God. God's word was unfaithfully disbelieved by a sinful man, and Gabriel's response appears to be one of shock. The quick lesson here is when God speaks, we should take him at his word regardless of how impossible it may sound. Yet there is more...

After observing Zechariah question the words of God, the spokesman of God then silenced the Lord's priest with dumbness until the Lord chose to

---

98 For a deeper review of "Naming a Child According to the Circumstances of Birth," see Zushe Wilhelm's contribution at: https://www.chabad.org/library/article_cdo/aid/273300/jewish/19-Naming-According-to-the-Circumstances-of-Birth.htm .
99 Dolores Smyth wrote a solid article at Crosswalk.com about "The Meaning and Importance of Biblical Names" at: https://www.crosswalk.com/faith/bible-study/why-are-names-so-important-in-the-bible.html
100 The others were Abraham and Sarah (Genesis 17:19); Abraham and Hagar (Genesis 16:11); Isaiah and his wife (Isaiah 8:3-4); Hosea and Gomer (1:4, 6, 9); & Joseph and Mary (Matthew 1:21).
101 See: https://www.behindthename.com/name/john
102 Luke 1:19; https://www.biblehub.com/luke/1-19.htm

fulfill his promise. The fulfillment was the birth of John, and John was to bring joy and delight into Zechariah's life. Interestingly, we can now derive another lesson from this passage. When we respond to God's grace with a dearth of faith, our joy and delight in him are silenced. How many times have you read a promise in the Bible or felt God leading you through a seemingly impossible situation, prayed about it, yet deep in your heart really questioned whether it would really happen? In a demonstration of my imperfectness, I admit that when I have prayed in the past, I have thought something along the line of, "Well, I don't really think this will happen since it has never happened before, but if it does, I'll be surprised then." When this occurs, we silence our joy by our own doing, but God declares "the joy of the Lord is our strength."[103] The one thing that is supposed to sustain us during trying and difficult times is silenced because of our lack of faith in God.

Understanding this concept led the apostle Paul to deduce the fact that when he (and we) are at our weakest points, this is when we must fully rely on the strength of God so that we will be our strongest. Zechariah's faith was weak at this time because decades had gone by and he and his wife never had a child. One can almost assuredly assume that the two of them had prayed and begged God for a child many times before, too. It was a culturally-observed curse not to have children and especially not to have a son. Zechariah and his wife were now old, which is a logical reason not to have the faith to believe you would have a child, but God demands our faith, not our logic. With man, some things are impossible; but with God, all things are possible[104] and Zechariah failed to remember who originally spoke the words being delivered by Gabriel.

We must never forget that the strength we need to make it through life must come from our joy in the Lord. Do not confuse joy with happiness. Happiness – like its opposite, anger – is a temporary and fleeting emotion. Joy, on the other hand, is a lifestyle given to us by the Holy Spirit when we become saved.[105] It is a promise[106] given to us by God as well as a command.[107] Yes, we are to live joyfully regardless of our circumstances. Jesus came to give us a joyous and abundant life,[108] and we need to be sure we live that way. How

---

103 Nehemiah 8:10; https://biblehub.com/nehemiah/8-10.htm
104 Matthew 19:26; https://www.biblehub.com/matthew/19-26.htm
105 Cf. Romans 14:17
106 Cf. Matthew 25:11
107 Cf. James 1:2
108 Cf. John 16:24

awesome a witness for Jesus is a Christian who demonstrates observable joy in his or her life even while going through terrible circumstances! Let us not silence our joy by turning an unfaithful ear toward God's Word and direction for our lives. After all, God promises to hear and answer our cries and prayers, and Christ rose from the dead so that we might walk in joy. We therefore need to rely less on what logically should happen according to how we see things and rely more so on a God who can do things that defy our logic.

FINITE OBSTACLES

Mankind's wisdom and logic during times we need to use our faith in Christ, Doubt, Forgetting that God is omnipotent

INFINITE TRUTH

God is indeed sovereign over all aspects of creation and ultimately has the final "say-so" over what comes about, even if our minds or circumstances try to tell us that he is not.

PRAYER

Dear Heavenly Father, "I will bless the Lord at all times. His praise shall continually be in my mouth." Help us to remain focused on you in faith regardless of our circumstances so that we may be a joyful witness to those around us. In Jesus' name, amen.

LESSON 12

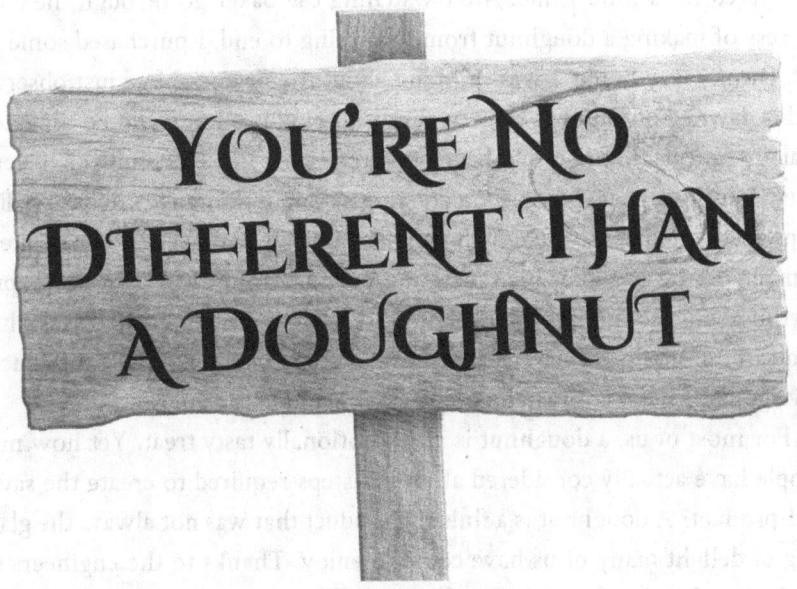

YOU'RE NO DIFFERENT THAN A DOUGHNUT

*"To man belong the plans of the heart,
but from the LORD comes the reply of the tongue."*

*"In his heart a man plans his course,
but the LORD determines his steps."*

PROVERBS 16:1 & 9

My wife and I used to drive down a certain major road close to where we once lived, and there was a Krispy Kreme doughnut store prominently placed alongside the road. After driving by the store numerous times and seeing the red, illuminated sign that declares "Hot Krispy Kreme's Now," I decided one day that I'd pull over and go inside. I had purchased Krispy Kreme doughnuts from fund raisers and at convenience stores before, but I had never actually gone inside one of their stores until that day. Once I got inside, I was quite surprised to see a glass wall that allowed for customers to watch the doughnut-making process, and I chose to stand and watch for a little while. After watching the baker go through the entire process of making a doughnut from beginning to end, I purchased some and left. On my way home, I was thinking about the process I had just observed, and it dawned on me that the doughnut-making process could be used as an analogy for certain times that have occurred in my life. Hopefully I'll never be eaten, but the process involved in creating a doughnut involves a lot of tedious steps that would cause the dough pain if it actually had nerve endings like we humans do. I know that inanimate ingredients cannot feel pain nor express anything, but the similarities of what those ingredients go through at the hand of a careful, master baker reminded me of some of the painful experiences I have gone through at the hand of my careful and masterful Lord.

For most of us, a doughnut is an exceptionally tasty treat. Yet how many people have actually considered all of the steps required to create the savory end-product? A doughnut is a finished product that was not always the glazed ring of delight many of us have come to enjoy. Thanks to the engineers and marketing department of the Krispy Kreme company, people are able to get a lesson in theology while waiting for some warm doughnuts to be made!

The baker first takes flour, yeast, sugar, and who knows what other ingredients and mixes them all into a sticky lump of dough. At this point, no one of a sound mind would consider eating this soft and shapeless lump of moist ingredients. Then the baker applies forceful pressure to the dough to flatten it. This reminds me of the many times God has had to "forcefully" apply pressure to my stubborn self in order to shape me the way he desires. There have even been times where the Lord has even had to "flatten" me too. While the dough can't feel these actions, I know and admit that this can be an uncomfortable process.

After the initial beating the dough takes, the baker then takes an air gun and actually shoots a high-velocity projectile of air right into the heart of the flattened lump of dough. Just like that, bang! the baker has removed the unwanted portion of the dough that would prevent it from turning out the way the master baker knows it should. When the unwanted material is finally removed, the dough is placed into an oven of high heat, which again re-shapes the doughnut from a flattened mass of nothingness with a hole ripped through it into a risen, soft ring that to an amateur would look appetizing. However, the baker is no amateur, and he would not allow the warm mass to be eaten because he knows it is not a finished product yet. If someone were to attempt to eat it at this time, it is likely that person would spit it out for lack of flavor.

While the once-sticky lump of ingredients now looks like a doughnut, it is still incomplete. It is then submerged – even drowned – in a blistering hot bath of oil, which utilizes the heat to solidify the character and body of the doughnut. The doughnut must then be removed from its searing bath of oil and allowed to drip off any excess so that the liquid doesn't prevent it from forming into a solid yet edible state. At this point, the doughnut again outwardly appears that it is ready for consumption, but it is still not quite finished yet. Finally, the baker takes the individual, perfectly formed, former lump of ingredients and applies sweet layers of glaze to it so that it will be ready for presentation and consumption. After all of the aforementioned work by the baker and all of the rough treatment the raw ingredients received, the process ultimately results in something worthy to an eager doughnut-lover.

We are really no different from a lump of ingredients, and God is no different than the master baker. While this sounds silly, the assortment of ingredients could (if it had a mind like we do) easily have desired to be a loaf of bread, a bagel, or a birthday cake, but that is not what the baker had in mind for the dough. The baker is the one tasked with the creating, shaping, and the ultimate end-purpose for the dough, and he puts the dough through all kinds of changes, trials, and re-shaping because the baker knows exactly what he seeks for the life of that specific lump of dough.

God also knows exactly what he wants for us and even tells us that he has an individualized plan for our lives.[109] Due to our sin-nature, we all tend to seek out our own plans for our lives even though God may have a different plan than we have. We really are similar to the raw ingredients bakers use to make doughnuts, as the Lord tells us that the first man was a finished product, made in the image of God[110] but out of the dust of the earth.[111] Since God is anything but passive over his creation[112] and is indeed sovereign,[113] we should expect that he will have a say in how we turn out. We can plan our course for life, but it is God who will determine our steps.[114] We may seek to do a particular thing

---

109 Jeremiah 29:11; https://biblehub.com/jeremiah/29-11.htm
110 Genesis 1:27; https://biblehub.com/genesis/1-27.htm
111 I Corinthians 15:47; https://www.biblehub.com/1_corinthians/15-47.htm
112 Cf. Deuteronomy 28:7-12
113 Job 42:2; https://www.biblehub.com/job/42-2.htm
114 Proverbs 16:9; https://biblehub.com/proverbs/16-9.htm

in life, but God sometimes has something different in store for us because he knows intricately how we were made, what gifts and talents we have, and how we can best be used for his glory. There are even times when our selfish desires can lead to death.[115] If we use our imagination, we can pretend that the lump of dough probably didn't like the flattening, the hole being blown through it, the cooking in an oven, and the boiling hot oil bath. We too do not like it when God places us in the crucible of life's trials to shape us into the child he calls us to be, but he does this because he loves us.[116] We are even told that when he disciplines us, we are blessed.[117]

Life is used by God to create us into a person who lets his light shine out through us. Notice that it is not our light, because we are but vessels.[118] The challenge to the scenario that we call life is to fish out God's plan for our lives from deep waters.[119] We are to submit to God's shaping of our lives while at the same time seeking to find out the manner in which God chooses to use us. I may never understand why God allowed my and Renee's two babies to die, but I do know he was sovereign over this tragedy in our lives. I also know for a fact that these two experiences yielded a number of fruits in our lives too. Both of these events almost resulted in a divorce, but God used our pain to maneuver us into a marriage retreat that radically changed our marriage. Renee and I learned communication tools we had never known at this retreat, and ever since then, she and I have had a strong, vibrant marriage. God also used these trials to create in us a heart for two impoverished children who live in the Dominican Republic. We sponsor two children born the same years we lost our children through Compassion International, and by doing so, these children are able to receive an education, have many of their physical needs met as well as hear the gospel of Jesus because the resource we use is devoted to doing these things. Renee and I were even able to fly down to the Dominican Republic and meet these two children and also see how this non-profit organization works. There are many other fruits I could list here, but I would prefer to have my readers reflect upon their own lives. What trials and severe tests has God put you through in order to shape you into a product worthy of his calling? There are

---

115 Cf. Proverbs 14:12
116 Compare Proverbs 3:12, Hebrews 12:6, Revelation 3:19, and Deuteronomy 8:5.
117 Psalm 94:12; https://biblehub.com/psalms/94-12.htm
118 Romans 9:21-23; https://www.biblegateway.com/passage/?search=Romans+9:21-23&version=NIV
119 Cf. Proverbs 20:5

so many available options of negativity in this world that we can focus on, but a blessed person is able to realize and acknowledge how God does indeed work all things for the good of those who love him and are called of him.[120]

Proverbs 8:32 and Proverbs 15:10 explain to us that God has a time-table for our lives, and the people who attempt to run ahead of it or lag behind it place themselves out of God's will and into harm's way. This is the very reason why it is imperative that we get in sync with God's plans, for they do not change,[121] cannot be thwarted,[122] stand firm forever,[123] and are better[124] than our own plans for our lives. Lastly, God informs us that the instruction he gives us through our ever-changing and often tumultuous lives yields his wisdom and *is* our life,[125] and those who accept his shaping of our lives, similar to the way a doughnut is shaped, will be honored,[126] stay on the right path,[127] and prosper.[128] So the next time you find yourself eating a doughnut or you find yourself dismayed at life's circumstances, remember, God puts us through all kinds of trials to test our faith, to make us righteous like him, and to prepare us to one day be a presentable bride to our Lord and Savior Jesus Christ.[129]

FINITE OBSTACLES

Humanity's limited perspective concerning both negative and positive events that occur in the world, A self-indulgent attitude especially when we face hardships

INFINITE TRUTH

God has a plan for every person's life, and he allows both positive and often negative events to occur to us so that we are directed to fulfill God's plans for us.

---

120 Romans 8:28; https://biblehub.com/romans/8-28.htm
121 Cf. Isaiah 14:24
122 Cf. Job 42:2
123 Cf. Psalm 33:11
124 Cf. Hebrews 11:40
125 Proverbs 4:13; https://biblehub.com/proverbs/4-13.htm
126 Cf. Proverbs 13:18
127 Cf. Proverbs 4:23
128 Cf. Proverbs 13:21
129 Cf. I Peter 1:6-7; II Corinthians 5:21; and Matthew 25:1-13

PRAYER

Heavenly Father, thank you for your wisdom that allows you to guide us, chastise us, and shape us into the person you desire. Please forgive us for our reluctance to trust you and our selfishness to fight your guidance. Please open our minds to the reality of how much you love us and want to bless us, and may it all be done for your glory. In Christ's name, amen.

LESSON 13

"Sing to the LORD! Give praise to the LORD! He rescues the life of the needy from the hands of the wicked."

JEREMIAH 20:13

The prophet Jeremiah offers us an example of how to respond to God amidst extremely tough life-circumstances. God called Jeremiah as his prophet to announce God's pending judgment on the Israelites due to their spiritual adultery. For the first twenty chapters of his book, Jeremiah faithfully announced God's truth even though it was painful even to him. He too was an Israelite and knew that he would somehow experience God's judgment on the nation since he lived there. Instead of hearing God's truths and running to hide from the prophesied and inevitable attacks from the

Babylonians, he instead went out, fulfilled God's plan for his life, and called for his fellow citizens to repent and turn back to God. Many of us have offered the hope of God's saving grace to others only for it to be rejected by a recalcitrant heart.

Jeremiah also experienced a rebellious reception from many he spoke with even to the point of being beaten and placed into stocks.[130] Just as we would probably hesitate to continue doing something that brings emotional and physical harm to us (in Jeremiah's case it was prophesying that did this), so too did Jeremiah go through a period of time where he questioned the value of doing what God called him to do because of the negative feedback he was receiving. Whenever he would choose not to do as God had instructed him, refusal resulted in "a fire in his bones"[131] that took so much strength to resist that he simply had to give in to it. This fiery feeling of conviction is what happens when God calls us to do something and we resist his calling. It tends to eat us up on the inside, but we have to grasp the whole of Jeremiah chapter twenty to find encouragement even when people discourage us.

I have also gone through a period of time where I resisted God's calling for my life, and I can confidently declare that I experienced a similar "fire" in my bones that ate me up on the inside. God called me to teach, and for about ten years I chose to refuse to follow God's calling on my life. It took so much strength to fight it. I tried many different jobs, idols, and alleged comforts, yet not one of them could provide the daily joy, contentment, and encouragement that I have experienced since submitting to God's will for my life as an educator. An added benefit that I never planned to experience while teaching is that I am now able to witness a desperate thirst for truth among both students and colleagues and then am able to be a conduit of the Lord to help quench that thirst. I count it a blessing to be able to see people hungering for something of substance, and when they learn the truth and how to think about it correctly, they just light up with life. It truly is a fulfillment of John 14:6.

Jesus told us that he is "the way, the truth, and the life," and when people learn "truth," they actually are learning about Christ for "in him all things are held together."[132] After a few years of watching the purported light come on in someone's head whenever they learned facts, I began to contemplate

---

130 Jeremiah 20:1-2; https://www.biblegateway.com/passage/?search=Jeremiah+20%3A1-2&version=NRSV
131 Jeremiah 20:9; https://biblehub.com/jeremiah/20-9.htm
132 Colossians 1:17; https://biblehub.com/colossians/1-17.htm

this phenomenon, asking the Lord for wisdom to understand it. I eventually realized that this enlightenment comes from truth, and as a result, I painted the Latin words above my door, *"Veritas Lux Mea"* (Truth Enlightens Me). What I learned was that if Christ *is* the truth as he declares, then it follows that all truth must logically flow from him. And if I teach truth, then I am essentially teaching Christ, just under a different idiom. And since Christ also declares he *is* life, it should not have been much of a shock to me when I witnessed people coming to life when they discovered the truth. This revelation radically transformed my teaching, which in turn, radically transformed my students. They began loving to come to my classroom because they loved the illumination that occurred inside its walls.

While many parents would comment to me that their child "loved my class," "came home and began talking about stuff they never discussed before," or that their child told them that I "was their favorite teacher," there were still detractors. There were times that my supervisors would inform me a parent had called them to complain about something I had said in class, but I observed the Lord fulfill Jeremiah 20:11-12 over and over again. My "persecutors stumbled and did not prevail" because I "committed my cause" to his (God's) purposes. As a result, the Lord rescued me from their attacks as well as the students from the assault on the very truth that they wanted (and needed) to hear. Both teacher and student were equally blessed, for the "needy were rescued" and as a result, I can declare "praise to the Lord!" in agreement with Jeremiah 20:13.

God has ensured us that our persecutors will stumble and not prevail over us, and we can be sure there will come a time when failure and disgrace will rest upon them if they do not repent. God sticks up for his children just as any of us would stick up for our own children. God even announced through Jeremiah that the dishonor we experience will never be forgotten.[133] What great news! What encouraging truths do we find from the experience of a persecuted, ancient prophet. Because of my own life circumstances, I can now state in agreement with Jeremiah that God does indeed rescue the needy from the hands of the wicked. How does he do that? On rare occasions, he does it miraculously, but most of the time God rescues mankind with truth – the very Word of God. Truth is what saves a person. Truth is what enlightens a person. Truth is what God is, and because of this, he will defend it and those who

---

133 Cf. Jeremiah 20:11

proclaim it because he is defending his very character and substance. He has rescued me from or through various persecutions, my own sin, and my own despair and insecurities. He has also enlightened us with the truth that others are out there simply waiting for us to screw up so that they can pounce on us, but God has promised to defend his children. Because of this, we can "sing to the Lord" and "give praise to the Lord," for we know that "He rescues the life of the needy from the hands of the wicked."

FINITE OBSTACLES

People who try to discourage you and your efforts,
Self-doubt, Ignorance of God's true character

INFINITE TRUTH

God will never leave us nor forsake us even when
it appears in our lives that he may have.

Prayer

Thank you, Lord, for your promise of protection even though it often comes through events rather than by the avoidance of events. Thank you for your Word and the faithfulness of your prophet Jeremiah, who gives us an example of obedience through persecution. Thank you for your truth, which overcomes all falsities. I ask that you continue to pour out your truth to the multitudes who thirst for it, and I ask you bless those willing to remain committed to telling your truth. In Jesus' name, amen.

LESSON 14

*"Do not envy the wicked, do not desire their
company; for their hearts plot violence,
and their lips talk about making trouble."*

PROVERBS 24:1-2

Proverbs chapter twenty-four is the last of the Proverbs that Solomon himself wrote and arranged. All others afterward were arranged under the supervision of Hezekiah. Knowing now that chapter twenty-four is King Solomon's "final words," and also understanding how most people really focus on meaningful comments when they are speaking for the last time to an audience, this should lead us to believe that Solomon starts off this chapter with wise advice that is truly heartfelt. Even a cursory observation of the world today reveals lots of terrible actions taking place by multitudes of people, and I think Solomon saw similar occurrences when he was alive. The sin-nature of humans is no worse now than when Solomon was living, and based on the fact that he warns against envying the wicked, I think he may be referencing his own personal struggle with a feeling that the wicked tend to get away with their depravity. We must remember that Solomon is credited with being one of the wisest men on earth, and his advice to us not to be envious of the wicked may sound like common sense at first, but how many times do you think people today and in times past have observed evil people do evil things and get away with it and think maybe they could too? This is that very envy that Solomon advises against.

I get utterly frustrated when I watch injustices appear to go unpunished. I bet you do too. When I look at the world around me, I cannot help but agree with Asaph, the author of Psalm 73, who honestly declared:

But as for me, my feet had almost slipped; I had nearly lost my foothold. For I envied the arrogant when I saw the prosperity of the wicked. They have no struggles; their bodies are healthy and strong. They are free from common human burdens; they are not plagued by human ills. Therefore pride is their necklace; they clothe themselves with violence. From their callous hearts comes iniquity; their evil imaginations have no limits. They scoff, and speak with malice; with arrogance they threaten oppression. Their mouths lay claim to heaven, and their tongues take possession of the earth. Therefore their people turn to them and drink up waters in abundance. They say, "How would God know? Does the Most High know anything?" This is what the wicked are like – always free of care, they go on amassing wealth. Surely in vain I have kept my heart pure and have washed my hands in innocence. All day long I have been afflicted, and every morning brings new punishments. If I had spoken out like that, I would have betrayed your children. When I tried to understand all this, it troubled me deeply till I entered the sanctuary of God; then I understood their final destiny.

I really like the honesty of Asaph, especially what he penned in verse thirteen, declaring that he "kept (his) heart pure in vain" for I can relate with his thoughts. I have witnessed people speak terrible lies about people and get away with it. I have seen television reports of heinous crimes having been committed only to watch the culprits somehow get away with it. I have lived long enough to realize that plenty of politicians commit unlawful acts yet somehow keep their jobs. While I could keep naming examples of wrongs seemingly going unpunished, my point is that I have also thought that trying to "keep my heart pure...in innocence was in vain." Thankfully we have the complete Word of God available to us because both Solomon and Asaph address the reality that no one actually gets away with their wickedness regardless of how life appears to us.

Solomon tells us not to envy the wicked because he understood God's unchanging, just character and knew that God settles all scores eventually. The prophet Isaiah informs us that God *will* punish the world for its wickedness.[134] Asaph asserts that he struggled with thinking bad people get away with bad things until he "entered the sanctuary of God" and ultimately realized "their final destiny." The final destiny of evil is a terrible topic to contemplate,[135] but it is assured by God's very words. God *will* deal with evil at some point, but until then, there is not much you and I can do about it because we cannot change a person's heart. All we can do is introduce them to the only one who can...Jesus. We can and should trust God to fulfill his word the times we drift off into thinking that crime pays off in the long-run.

Instead of being envious of the wicked, our focus should be on what God has called us to do in our own lives. We will be much happier when our focus changes to our own responsibilities. We can, like Asaph, tell God what frustrates us, but we must go on with our lives and trust God to work justice out in his perfect timing. If we can get ourselves to the point where we think about life from God's point of view, then the many examples of wicked people doing wicked acts won't make us very envious of them. Even the righteous cannot get away with sin. Consider the following examples of people who appeared to have gotten away with crime, and then weigh that against their ultimate ending:

---

134 Isaiah 13:11; https://biblehub.com/isaiah/13-11.htm
135 Cf. Hebrews 10:31

- Cain killed Abel, but what happened to Cain? He was banished from the very few people who dwelled on the earth at that time.

- David had an affair with Bathsheba and arranged for her husband's murder, but what happened to David? His and Bathsheba's son was taken from them, and David wasn't allowed to build God's temple.

- Abimelech was terrible towards his people, even murdering the entire town of Shechem, but he had to beg a servant to kill him after his skull was crushed by a dropped stone.

- Athaliah, daughter of the notorious Ahab and Jezebel, allowed sacred objects to be used in Baal worship and killed all but one of David's male descendants. She had a short reign and was ultimately killed by her guards.

- It looked like the Persian Haman was going to get away with genocide of all of the Jews, but he was hanged on the very gallows he had built for a Jewish man.

- The Anti-Christ will have a temporary reign of terror but will ultimately end up in the Lake of Fire.

The Apostle Paul, just like Solomon and Asaph, recognized that thinking evil people will get away with their wrong-doings is sheer deception. God will not be mocked. Man will reap what he sows.[136] We too should be encouraged not to fall for such deceit either and instead concentrate on fulfilling our life's calling through the power of the Holy Spirit. Doing so will help prevent us from worrying about things that only God can control.

---

136 Galatians 6:7; https://biblehub.com/galatians/6-7.htm

FINITE OBSTACLES

Worry, Focusing on what others do rather than what we are responsible to do, Disbelief in God's sovereignty

INFINITE TRUTH

God will reward the righteous and punish the wicked. It just might not occur on our preferred timeline.

PRAYER

Heavenly Father, we thank you today for your sovereignty over all the affairs of this world. While many events seem to occur that are frustrating and unjust, we know you are a just God who will settle all scores eventually. Thank you for this fact, and may we always remember this the times we feel tempted to envy the wicked. In the name of our Lord and Savior, Jesus Christ, amen.

LESSON 15

GOD SOMETIMES DESTROYS HIS OWN ALTAR

> *I saw the Lord standing by the altar, and he said:*
> *"Strike the tops of the pillars*
> *so that the thresholds shake.*
> *Bring them down on the heads of all the people;*
> *those who are left I will kill with the sword.*
> *Not one will get away,*
> *none will escape.*
> *"Surely the eyes of the Sovereign LORD*
> *are on the sinful kingdom.*

> *I will destroy it*
> *from the face of the earth—*
> *yet I will not totally destroy*
> *the house of Jacob,"*
> *declares the LORD.*
> *All the sinners among my people*
> *will die by the sword,*
> *all those who say,*
> *'Disaster will not overtake or meet us.'*
> *"In that day I will restore*
> *David's fallen tent.*
> *I will repair its broken places,*
> *restore its ruins,*
> *and build it as it used to be,*
>
> AMOS 9:1, 8, 10, 11

St. Louis Cardinals baseball is very much a part of the St. Louis-area culture. Most of us from that area grow up "loving" the Cardinals and "hating" the Chicago Cubs. Furthermore, many young boys and some girls grow up playing the game of baseball and grow to love the game as well and many learn to play it. I was one of those young boys, but rather than acknowledging that baseball was a game to be enjoyed, I am ashamed to say that it became my idol. Baseball consumed my life as a young man to the point where I failed to acknowledge God as my source of security and I foolishly placed all of my hopes in the game of baseball. As I stated, part of the culture of being a St. Louisan is baseball, but this cultural influence became a stumbling block that prevented me from fulfilling God's will for my life for a long time.

When studying the ancient Hebrew culture found within the text of the Bible, one of the main cultural influences for the Hebrew people was the altar, which was where ceremonial worship of God took place. Just as cheering for the Cardinals is commonplace to many of us from St. Louis, so too was "cheering" for God and worshiping him at the altar commonplace for the Jewish nation. However, the book of Amos is an account of God's announcement of judgment on the northern kingdom of Israel. For those of you not as familiar with the north-south split of the Israelite nation,[137] after King Solomon died, his twelve-tribe kingdom was split into two. Ten of the tribes comprised the northern Kingdom of Israel, which was ruled by only wicked kings; while two tribes comprised the southern kingdom, which was called the Kingdom of Judah. It was ruled off-and-on by both good kings and bad ones.

The book of Amos was written around 750 B.C. so the altar is very much a prominent aspect of Jewish culture at this time. God is found in verse one of Amos chapter nine to be standing by this cultural center of the Israelites...the altar. God tells Amos to announce that God will "strike the pillars and bring them down on the heads of all the people." Additionally, verses two through four summarize the totality of God's judgment, which was complete. This begs the question, "Why would God destroy the very altar where his chosen people were to worship him?" As mentioned above, my altar was a diamond where the game of baseball was played, and I mistakenly thought it was I who determined my destiny. I always felt a nudge deep within my heart that I was mismanaging my priorities, but I kept on in my self-centered ways until one day, God announced judgment on my idolatry just as he did on the Israelites. God began his judgment at his own altar because that was the very source of security of the Israelite people. God destroyed it because it was their main focus rather than God. They expected to find peace and security at the altar. It was where they received and gave blessings and offerings as well. God, by standing by Israel's altar and announcing his destruction of it, and by declaring no one will escape his judgment, was destroying the Israelite basis of false security so that they would turn back to God as their authentic base of security and draw near to him. He created people to live in communion with him. The Israelites had fallen so far away from God and had allowed cultural ritualism to become their idols that God lovingly yet sternly had to destroy what was keeping his people from fulfilling his will for their lives.

God did this in my life as well. He slowly began to remove my idolatry of baseball out of my heart through the destruction first of my dedication to

---

137 See I Kings chapters 11 and 12 for the details of the bifurcation of Solomon's kingdom.

play the game, then through the destruction of my shoulder and elbow, and finally, one year he graciously removed any inward desire to play or coach it. I resigned from my coaching position and began giving away all of my articles of idol-worship to some of the kids I coached. What once dominated my life and became a spiritual hindrance from fulfilling God's will for my life, God lovingly destroyed so that I could get into a right relationship with him. However, we also read in Amos 9:8 that God "will not totally destroy the House of Jacob (the northern kingdom)." God did not completely remove baseball from my life either, as I still enjoy being a fan of the Cardinals, and God allowed me to remain around the game and blessed me for years with an income as an umpire for high school and college baseball games. We still need to beware though, as God does include a caveat for those who resist his destruction of idols: Verse ten declares that those who resist by stating, "Disaster will not overtake us..." will in fact "die by the sword." Thankfully I escaped the sword, but many Israelites did not, as the Assyrians sacked their kingdom in 722 B.C.

As we finally come to verse eleven, we see how God's love occurs even through his judgment. God promised future generations that "he will restore David's fallen tent" and "repair and restore" the broken down ruins. This Messianic prophesy ensured the Israelites that he would keep the covenant he made with King David and always keep one of his descendants on the throne.[138] We now know that descendant was/is Jesus Christ, our Messiah.[139] He sits on the eternal throne at the right hand of God.[140] I had lost sight of God for a long time in my life. I idolized baseball and myself, and God loved me enough to destroy my source of idolatry while sparing my life. When Jesus hung on the cross of Calvary, he bore the judgment for my sin and died in my place (Hallelujah!). The Israelites of the eighth century B.C. also lost sight of God and his plan for their lives. They became carefree and comfortable with their sin and simply observed cultural rituals instead of truly loving God as he dictated they should.

We cannot allow anything in our lives to take our focus off of God as our source of security, comfort, blessing, and Lordship. We also must learn the lesson the northern kingdom had to learn the hard way, which was that going to church (in their case the altar) and "being good" is not good enough for

---

138 Cf. 2 Samuel 7:12-16; 1 Chronicles 17:11-15
139 Cf. Matthew 1:1; Luke 1:32-33; Acts 15:15-16; Hebrews 1:15
140 Cf. Luke 22:69; Romans 8:34; Colossians 3:1; Hebrews 12:12

Holy God. We must allow – even invite – God to penetrate every aspect of our lives, for anything that we hold back from his penetration is an idol. Ask the Lord today to show you any areas of your life that may be a hindrance to your relationship with him. Ask him to reveal to you any idols you may knowingly or unknowingly have placed before him. We need to re-examine our spiritual health every so often so that we can live faithfully according to God's will for our lives, and it is then that we will experience joy and security.

FINITE OBSTACLES
Idols

INFINITE TRUTH
Only the triune God is God. Everything else that we place before him is an idol.

Prayer

Thank you Lord that you love us enough to destroy that which keeps us from a right-relationship with you. Thank you for repairing the sinful fracture between us and you with your son Jesus and his faithful work of the cross. In Christ's name, amen.

LESSON 16

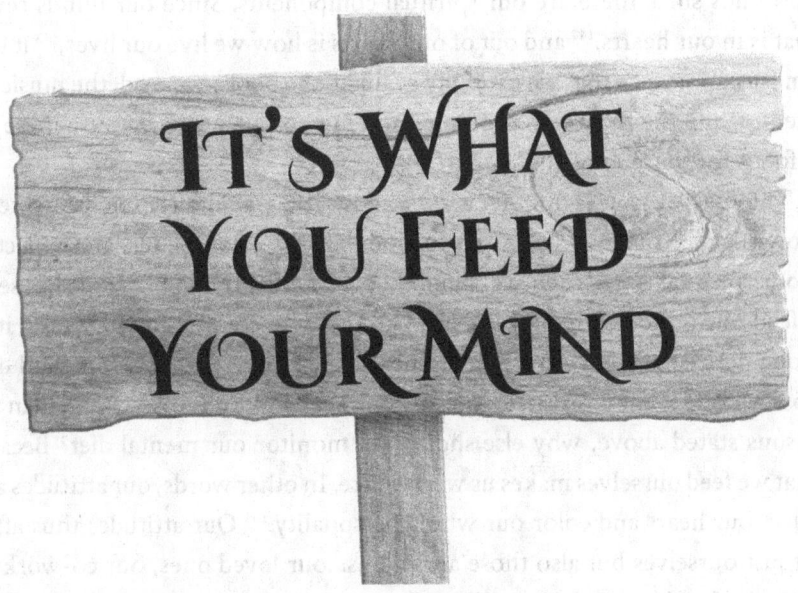

"The discerning heart seeks knowledge, but the mouth of a fool feeds on folly. All the days of the oppressed are wretched, but the cheerful heart has a continual feast."

PROVERBS 15:14-15

A common truth known and experienced by most adults is that as we age, it becomes harder and harder to manage our weight. Doing so requires a consistent monitoring of what we feed our bodies. We have all been told or have heard another person say that continually feeding on unhealthy food results in an unhealthy body. Every time I step on a scale, the veracity of this statement seems confirmed. You may also have heard another true statement that declares, "As it is in the physical realm, so too is it in the spiritual realm."[141] We can therefore conclude that maintaining a healthy spiritual life requires us to carefully monitor what we feed our hearts and minds since these are our spiritual components. Since our minds reveal what is in our hearts,[142] and out of our hearts is how we live our lives,[143] it is of utmost importance that we carefully evaluate the books we read, the music we listen to, and the television programs and movies we watch because these are all foods for our mental diet.

The Lord conveys in the verses above that a "discerning heart seeks knowledge..." It is then honoring to God, healthy to our souls, and reflective of our spiritual state when we maintain a perpetual frame of mind that seeks to feed our minds with God's Word and the wise counsel found within it. A strong desire to discover truth and knowledge is a mark of wisdom, and only those who fear the Lord truly can begin to attain wisdom.[144] Other than the reasons stated above, why else should we monitor our mental diet? Because what we feed ourselves makes us who we are. In other words, our attitudes also reflect our heart and color our whole personality.[145] Our attitudes thus affect not just ourselves but also those around us...our loved ones, our co-workers, those the Lord brings into our lives for ministry, etc. Have you ever run into someone who acted a certain way or treated people in ways with which you disagreed and thought, "Geez, that guy/gal must be miserable on the inside?" The reason you may have thought or said this is because you already grasped some of the truth being described above. We become just like that which we put into ourselves both physically and mentally. This should give us pause so that we evaluate our own diets.

We cannot always choose what happens to us, and most of the time we have absolutely no control over such events,[146] but we can choose our attitude and response to each situation set before us. To maintain a positive and cheerful heart, it then becomes imperative that we follow the apostle Paul's advice and continually fill our hearts/minds with thoughts and images of truth, purity, love, and things that dwell on the blessings (good things) of life.[147] We need to

---

141 Cf. I Corinthians 15:44
142 Proverbs 23:7; https://biblehub.com/kjv/proverbs/23-7.htm
143 Proverbs 27:19; https://biblehub.com/kjv/proverbs/27-19.htm
144 Cf. Proverbs 1:7 and 9:10.
145 Cf. Philippians 4:8-9
146 Cf. Proverbs 16:1
147 Philippians 4:8; https://biblehub.com/philippians/4-8.htm

examine our attitudes and what we feed our minds. We need to do a "check-up from the neck up" in order to determine if what we are dwelling on is truly profitable[148] and yields a "cheerful heart." Christ promises us that his burden is light and that he will give us rest when we take up that burden and focus on his gentleness and teachings.[149] This is not only healthy to our physical and spiritual bodies, it also honors God with the time and gifts he gave us and it will give us the ability to discern what is truly important and what is a waste of our time. Take some time soon to complete a "check-up from the neck up" and make sure you are feeding your mind positive and healthy information so that your thoughts produce the fruit of the Spirit.[150]

FINITE OBSTACLES

Spiritual junk food, Unwholesome images and words, A lack of focus on Christ

INFINITE TRUTH

Due to our inherited sin-natures, we need to periodically evaluate our mental and spiritual diets, repent, and ensure we are focused on what is important so that in Christ, we can "be holy as (Christ) is holy."[151]

---

148 Cf. II Timothy 3:16
149 Matthew 11:28-30; https://www.biblegateway.com/passage/?search=Matthew+11%3A28-30&version=ESV
150 Cf. Galatians 5:22-23
151 I Peter 1:15-16; https://www.biblegateway.com/passage/?search=1+Peter+1%3A15-16&version=NIV

Prayer

May the Lord reveal to us those things that are not profitable to our lives, and may we remain faithful to him when he blesses us with the uncomfortable yet beneficial fires of reproof. In Jesus' name, amen.

LESSON 17

"You of this generation, consider the word of the Lord:"

JEREMIAH 2:31

This is going to be a very tough lesson to read because it is convicting. I think everyone who reads these words (myself included) will find that God's justice balances his love. There are a lot of churches that simply preach a "feel-good" gospel...one that focuses on God's incredible love and his grace. However, those are not the only two qualities the Bible tells us about our Creator. The Old Testament is full of stories about God's own chosen people being reprimanded for sin, which is what makes the true account of the gospel so much sweeter than it already is. You see, millennia went by where God's people had his law. They had his presence.[152] They had promises and covenants and numerous examples in the past where God upheld his own people. Yet we read time and again that those same people continued to sin, turn their backs on God despite his mercy and grace, suffer judgment, repent, and then do it all over again. These stories serve as examples to us that mankind desperately needs a savior because of the damning effects of cyclical sin.

After King Solomon died, the nation of Israel split into two. The northern kingdom was known as Israel and the southern kingdom became known as Judah. The prophet Jeremiah was called by God when he was a young man for the specific purpose of "uprooting and tearing down, destroying and overthrowing, and building and planting" in Judah.[153] He served as God's spokesman to Judah for forty years, and throughout this period of time he suffered death threats, persecutions, and wept desperately for his own people. He loved his nation and understood its history. He was well-aware of how God delivered her out of the hands of the Egyptians, and Jeremiah's message was a consistent and passionate call for the Hebrew people to turn away from their idolatrous sin and return to God. Failure to do so, as God revealed clearly to Jeremiah, will (and did) result in God passing judgment on Judah. The nation of Babylon conquered the southern kingdom in 586 B.C. and carried off its remaining inhabitants into servitude and slavery. Throughout Jeremiah's ministry, he kept reminding the Judeans of their past. He kept calling to memory how God worked in their lives and the lives of their ancestors. He recalled[154] how God faithfully protected them, nourished them, and guided them, and he also called to their attention how they were currently sinning by turning their backs on God even though he remained faithful[155] throughout the decades. God's message as spoken through the mouth of Jeremiah was for the people to turn from their wicked ways (repent) and again serve God. Doing so was God's will and would result in restoration. However, as history proved, Judah failed to heed God's multiple warnings and it was destroyed in God's judgment.

Since this verse from Jeremiah above addresses its readers as "You of this generation..." we can conclude that regardless of the time a person reads this verse, that person falls into the category of a "you" of his/her own generation.

---

152 Cf. Exodus 13:21, 40:34-35; I Kings 8:10-11
153 Jeremiah 1:10; https://biblehub.com/jeremiah/1-10.htm
154 Cf. Jeremiah 2:2
155 Cf. Deuteronomy 7:9; Psalm 89:1; I Corinthians 1:9

It then follows that this command of God to "consider the word of the Lord" applies to all people in all cultures at any time. This verse calls out to anyone who lives in a rebellious and spiritually adulterous generation, and based on the examples God gives us that reveal spiritual adultery, we can easily conclude that our nation is one of many that should heed this warning. America, like the nation of Judah, was set apart for its devotion to the Living God who is our Creator.[156] Its stated principles were founded upon God-inspired promises and commands.[157] Judah, like America, prospered for many years because it served God. However, Judah allowed itself to become entangled with foreigners who introduced their idols into Judean society and Judah turned to spiritual prostitution as a result. America is also falling into similar harlotry, with many of our people worshipping the idols of wealth, power, environmentalism, and alliances instead of Jesus. Can America expect God to address her any differently than he did his own chosen people?

God is not a God who forgets.[158] In fact, God urges us to recall history as can be seen in at least one hundred references in the Bible.[159] He calls us not to forget. Forgetting is dangerous whether it is intentional or an innocent oversight, for doing so prevents us from measuring our growth that has been enabled in history by God's grace, goodness, and his discipline. The more we focus on the passing pleasures of this life, the easier it is to forget what God has said and done. When we forget God, we then focus on any sort of idol, and we are therefore no longer concentrating on truth. America's history is one of God's love, his dependability and guidance, and most of all, God himself. Our national motto is "In God We Trust." Forgetting our past makes it easy to forget God. This is why it is imperative that American children are taught the true roots of this nation. This is why it is paramount that our children know the fundamental principles upon which our *Declaration* and *Constitution* were based. This is why we need modern Christians to remind the people that God does not take spiritual idolatry lightly. The Lord allowed his own people to be destroyed and their culture absolutely exasperated, and America is teetering on a similar tight-wire. We need to remember our Lord and come

---

156 See *The Declaration of Independence*, Thomas Jefferson; https://www.goodreads.com/quotes/675958-we-hold-these-truths-to-be-self-evident-that-all-men
157 For a more in-depth treatment of this assertion, consider Mark David Hall, *The Old Puritan and a New Nation: Roger Sherman and the Creation of the American Republic*, chapter 3. Also consider the David Barton article "Is America a Christian Nation?" at https://wallbuilders.com/america-christian-nation/
158 Cf. Hebrews 6:10
159 For a list on one hundred Biblical references calling for people to "remember," see: https://www.openbible.info/topics/remembering

back to our God, America! It is time for us to remember the writings of our Founders, repent of our transgressions, and return to the Creator God named in our founding documents.

FINITE OBSTACLES

Amnesia, Rebellion; A foolish insistence of operating our way rather than God's way

INFINITE TRUTH

While most Americans will argue that the form of republican government our Founding Fathers gave us is good, no government – regardless of its type – can succeed without an acknowledgment of God.

Prayer

Revive our hearts, oh Lord. Forgive us and cleanse our nation. Heal us of our physical and spiritual ailments wrought by a hedonistic lifestyle. Restore our national confidence in you, for we have turned away from the spring of Living Water and turned instead to broken cisterns of dust. Our wickedness is before you, and you are not unjust, oh Lord. Bring a revival first within your church and then among our countrymen. Have mercy on our nation, Lord Jesus, and may God once again bless America.

LESSON 18

You Are in the Lineup for a Specific Purpose

> "'Before I formed you in the womb I knew you,
> before you were born I set you apart; I appointed
> you as a prophet to the nations'."
>
> "But the LORD said to me, 'Do not say, I am only
> a child. You must go to everyone I send you to
> and say whatever I command you.'"
>
> "Get yourself ready! Stand up and say to them
> whatever I command you. Do not be terrified by
> them, or I will terrify you before them'."
>
> JEREMIAH 1:5, 7, 17

As an education administrator, I speak with many students who have various forms of struggles. Many of the students I see for behavior-related reasons have any number of challenges that complicate their education. Some are affected by poverty; some by trauma. Some are affected by their hormonal changes. Many allow the ups-and-downs of relationships to affect them. A lot of them struggle with a combination of the above and much more, but one common denominator I frequently hear through conversations with these representatives of the next generation is a struggle with self-doubt. It is a terrible thing to hear children declare something along the lines that they have no value, wish they were not alive, or tell me that they "hate themselves." It is heartbreaking, and I have often wondered if these same children have ever told their parents what they tell me. And if they have in fact told their parents these heartbreaking statements, I wonder what occurs behind closed doors that makes these kids feel this way. I will never be privy to much of that information, but I do know all people have value because they were created in the image of God.[160] I also know that this very same God has an individual plan[161] and calling[162] for each one of these dear children, and I reckon that if they heard those words instead of many of the cultural platitudes they likely hear, they would likely have a better outlook.

When one reads the message of the above passages and allows it to deeply sink into one's heart, it becomes one of the most powerful in all of scripture. God, the righteous, holy, majestic, omnipotent Creator of all things who sits on the throne of heaven actually thought about each and every one of us even before we were conceived! Prior to our parents meeting each other, God identified a specific call for each and every one of us and set it into motion by enabling our conception and birth! There is not much dispute that conception is truly a miracle, and when one considers what God has to say about it, it becomes clear that he performs that miracle and gives children to parents so that the child can eventually fulfill a task that God mapped out in heaven for him or her. What joy it should be then to parents to know that the child God miraculously presented to them is known by God and has a specific plan laid out in the heavens by the Creator-God!

---

160 Genesis 1:27; https://biblehub.com/genesis/1-27.htm
161 Cf. Jeremiah 29:11
162 Cf. II Timothy 1:9; Ephesians 1:4

God declared to Jeremiah while he was very young that he was set apart specifically as a prophet. God, in verse seven, responds to Jeremiah's hesitancy to his call by telling Jeremiah not to give him any excuses and then commanding him to "go to everyone I send you to and say what I command you to say." Verses eight and seventeen record God's encouragement to Jeremiah because of his fear of such a calling: "Do not be afraid of (the people I send you to), for I am with you and will rescue you." "Get yourself ready! Stand up and say to them whatever I command you. Do not be terrified by them, or I will terrify you before them."

The Message translation of verse 17 is foreboding, for it warns all of us (since all of us have a specific calling in life):

〰〰〰〰〰〰〰〰〰〰〰〰〰〰〰〰〰〰〰〰〰〰〰〰〰〰〰〰〰〰

"But you—up on your feet and get dressed for work!
Stand up and say your piece. Say exactly what I tell you to say.
Don't pull your punches or I'll pull you out of the lineup."

〰〰〰〰〰〰〰〰〰〰〰〰〰〰〰〰〰〰〰〰〰〰〰〰〰〰〰〰〰〰

Since God designed a plan for all of our lives prior to our conception, it is no wonder that God threatens to "pull us out of the lineup" if we don't heed his calling. He promises to be with us every place he calls us to go.[163] He promises to rescue us from every threat that arises. We should therefore boldly pronounce the words that God places in our mouths because it is God himself who places those words into our mouths.[164] We should also set our hearts[165] to desire God's will for our lives, because the Word is clear that our natural desires[166] are sinful. Let us boldly fulfill the plans that God designed for our lives. Whatever work you are called to do should be done for the glory of God.[167] If God gives you a specific task, call, duty, or assignment, then accept it cheerfully and obediently and do it with faithful diligence. If you are unsure of what God has set you apart to do, then diligently fulfill the mission that is common to all Christians: to love,[168] obey,[169] and to serve[170] the Lord until his mission for your life becomes clear.

---

163 Cf. Deuteronomy 4:31, 31:6; Psalm 37:25; II Corinthians 4:9
164 Jeremiah 1:9; https://biblehub.com/jeremiah/1-9.htm
165 Romans 8:4-6; https://www.biblegateway.com/passage/?search=Romans+8:4-6&version=NIV
166 Cf. Romans 6:12
167 Matthew 5:16; https://biblehub.com/matthew/5-16.htm
168 John 13:34-35; https://www.biblegateway.com/passage/?search=John+13:34-35
169 Jeremiah 7:23; https://biblehub.com/jeremiah/7-23.htm
170 Acts 1:8; https://biblehub.com/acts/1-8.htm

FINITE OBSTACLES
Laziness, Hesitancy, Fear, Confusion

INFINITE TRUTH
God is not the author of confusion, and he has a plan for you which is good and to prosper you. Take inventory of the gifts and talents he's given you and get into the game!

PRAYER

Dear Lord, please open our hearts to your will for our lives. Give us ears to hear your calling set forth for our lives. Provide in us the ability to hear your will and place the words you seek us to speak in our mouths. Give us the strength and courage to fulfill your calling in our lives, and encourage us when fear tempts us to turn from your will. In the name of Jesus, amen.

LESSON 19

SOMETIMES IT'S THEIR REACTION THAT MATTERS.

> "Adam lay with his wife Eve, and she became pregnant and gave birth to Cain. She said, 'With the help of the Lord I have brought forth a man.' Later she gave birth to his brother Abel. Now Abel kept flocks, and Cain worked the soil. In the course of time Cain brought some of the fruits of the soil as an offering to the Lord. But Abel brought fat portions from some of the firstborn of his flock. The Lord looked with favor on Abel and his offering, but on Cain and his offering he did not look with favor. So Cain was very angry, and his face was downcast."
>
> "Now Cain said to his brother Abel, 'Let's go out to the field.' While they were in the field, Cain attacked his brother Abel and killed him."
>
> GENESIS 4:1-5, 8

Two seemingly unrelated events occurred in my life that have helped to reveal the wisdom contained in the above verses in Genesis. One occurred over a year-long period of time before I entered the Navy. The other one occurred around twenty years later while I was a teacher and coach.

When I was nineteen years of age, I had the privilege of living with my two God-fearing grandparents for a year before entering the U.S. Navy. God used that time to teach me how a righteous man (my grandfather) is supposed to carry himself. I remember many times listening to conversations between my grandparents where they were discussing how someone at their church or one of my grandfather's students were blessed by the Lord somehow. My grandfather many times would respond how great that was or comment, "Good for so-and-so." I also remember thinking back then, "Why in the world is my grandpa happy for them? Why is he rejoicing when God blesses someone else?" Those questions were finally answered some years later.

After my "playing days" were over as a baseball player, I had always had a goal of coaching baseball at the high school level. I was honored to have been able to achieve that goal early in my teaching career, but after three years of doing so, I resigned from my coaching position. Throughout a difficult and challenging year, I would confide with a person in whom I trusted. We discussed many of my heart-felt fears and frustrations, and I would often share with that person some of the blessings I would receive from the Lord. Later on, however, I discovered that some of my words spoken in confidentiality were actually being shared with others behind my back and to my detriment. After a careful evaluation of our history, some of the comments made to me by this person, and other previous actions taken by this person, some members of my family and I were able to reasonably conclude that my confidant was in fact not rejoicing with me when God blessed me. He was instead witnessing my success, but his face evidently "became downcast" as Cain's once did. It is very possible that this person had ill-will in mind for me all along, and I trusted someone who was not really trustworthy. Due to my likely error in character-judgment, I allowed myself to be placed into a position where this person's comments resulted in me deciding it would be best for me to move on. I ultimately gave up a one-time dream due to the damage this person had done, and I suspect you've probably gone through a similar situation at some point in your life.

On the very same day I resigned, I also had a conversation with one of my students who also happened to play baseball for me. This young man came to my classroom toward the end of the school day and told me that his mother was taking him to get his driver's permit after school. About two or three hours later, I received a text message from him declaring that he "just got (his) driver's permit!" I recall experiencing an instant feeling of joy entering my heart on his behalf for his success. I replied back to him a message that rejoiced with him for the blessing that God brought into his life, but I did not realize that the Lord was also using that moment to teach me a life lesson as well.

We read above that Abel was blessed by God with acknowledgment and acceptance for bringing God a sacrifice. Abel did no harm toward his brother Cain and in fact was only doing God's will, yet his brother became angry with Abel to the point of killing him instead of rejoicing with him for receiving God's blessing. A difficult lesson all of us have to learn at some point is that there are people in our lives who we can trust and many people who we cannot. That may sound like "common sense," but nothing is common if we do not learn it. Those that we can trust can be identified by how they react when God blesses us. It is easy for someone to feel sorry for another person when bad things occur in a person's life. There are many of our acquaintances who will say something to us or help us out when we are downcast. However, the selfish nature of a sinful human makes it much harder for them to be excited for another person when they are blessed by God due to jealousy.

We need to be very cognizant of who we select to be in our inner circle.[171] We need to carefully observe how people react when the Lord brings blessings into our lives because it is during these times that people reflect what is in their heart. A righteous person who has true, God-like love in their heart will rejoice with those who God blesses because they love God and understand that the source of all blessings is God.[172] Due to this, jealousy is minimized because their heart is focused on God rather than themselves. This is the reason my grandfather was consistently able to rejoice with others when they were blessed. He was focused on God, not himself.

When we put our trust in people who are not focused on God but rather on themselves, their sinful hearts go to work at scheming against others for their own personal gain. It appears that I fell prey to such an action; however,

---

171 Cf. Proverbs 14:15
172 Cf. Psalm 24:5

I rejoice in the Lord for that situation because it actually served to make me a better man. I hold no ill-will in my heart for this person who betrayed me. I was able to forgive this person but it was only because Jesus has forgiven me and I am commanded to do the same. If it were up to my own sinful nature, I likely would have sought revenge. Nevertheless, it was exciting that the Lord used a painful event in my life to teach me how to identify a true, God-centered friend through this situation. I knew that if it was God's will for my life that if I ever coached high school baseball again, he would be the one who would appoint me to that position.[173]

I now thank the Lord today for loving me enough to use my grandfather and a rough, temporary time in my life to teach me the eternal lesson that sometimes a person's reactions do matter. It is very likely that you have also been in a similar situation where you misplaced trust in someone else. Rather than harboring anger in your heart, consider that experience a moment where you were placed in a position to learn forgiveness. After all, every one of us is guilty of betraying our Creator through sin, yet he still loved us enough to offer us an opportunity to be forgiven.[174]

FINITE OBSTACLES
Jealousy, Anger, Self-focus, Envy

INFINITE TRUTH

While we were yet jealous, angry, and self-serving sinners, Christ still died for us. Because God chooses to love others and bless them, we too should choose to be excited for our brothers and sisters in Christ when God blesses them and shun the envy that naturally raises its head when this occurs.

---

173 Cf. Psalm 75:7
174 Romans 5:8; https://biblehub.com/romans/5-8.htm

PRAYER

Dear Lord, thank you for loving us enough to use all events in our lives to help us grow regardless of whether they are positive or negative experiences. Thank you for teaching us how to forgive people, and thank you for information in your Word that that helps us select friends. Please bless us with the ability to love others enough to share their joy with them, and give us opportunities to share these lessons with others so that you might be glorified in the future. In Jesus' name, amen.

Lesson 20

> *"Then the word of the LORD came to Elijah: 'Leave here, turn eastward and hide in the Kerith Ravine, east of the Jordan. You will drink from the brook, and I have ordered the ravens to feed you there'."*
>
> I KINGS 17:2-4

How many times in your life have you obeyed God's calling in your life to go somewhere and then received his blessings as a result? You may have physically moved from a physical point "A" to point "B," or you may have simply moved out of a behavior or mindset into a different one. Perhaps God moved you out of one relationship and into another? Regardless of what that "movement" involved, we can be sure that God is in the moving business.[175]

When I was in high school, I felt the Lord calling me to teach, but I had other plans. I was going to play baseball at first, but then my shoulder became damaged. Due to the injured shoulder, I had spent so much time in physical therapy that I decided I was then going to become a physical therapist. However, when I contacted the (at that time) four universities that offered physical therapy degrees in my home state, I was told that I'd be placed on a four-year waiting list to even begin the program! I recall thinking at that time that it would be foolish for me to go to college for four years to get an undergraduate degree only to have to start a second undergraduate degree once I finished the first one. The thought of this (avoidable) predicament was very discouraging to my immature mind at the time, so I ended up joining the U.S. Navy.

When I joined the Navy, this pretty much ended my ability to go to physical therapy school, so I focused on being the best sailor I could be. Then I got married and sought to live the life of a family man, yet the Navy did not offer very good monetary means to support my family. Due to this, I ended up attempting to earn more money through working additional aimless jobs. While this did provide a larger income for my household, I exited the Navy and then ended up working two and sometimes three jobs at a time just to keep our heads "above water." This period of time in my life of working sixty to eighty-hour work-weeks can be visualized by imagining an orange fishing bobber just being tossed about on an unsettled body of water. Eventually, that "bobber" (my metaphorical head) went under that water, and I could no longer stay afloat myself. The whole time this was occurring, I still felt God calling me to get my teaching degree and certificate. After moving from one job to the next and from one area to another, I finally began taking education classes and Satan began to resist the Lord's working in my life on the spiritual level.

Operating in a similar manner to the way he did in the Garden of Eden, Satan began by attacking my then-wife. Furthermore, he then made attempts to hinder my teaching career even before it could take flight. While all of this was occurring, God called me back to St. Louis, for it was there that he

---

[175] The following link will give the reader one hundred different Bible verses that reference "moving." https://www.openbible.info/topics/moving

would supply all of my needs and miraculously work to fulfill his plans for my life. I am now an educator, and God has blessed me spiritually, emotionally, vocationally, and even inspirationally while being enabled to make a difference in the lives of my students and our nation by extension. I have found success in education, but even better than that, I have found a peace and a joy now that I am fulfilling God's role for my life.

If you read the entire context found in I Kings chapter seventeen, you will find that God was judging his people and its leader, King Ahab. God's means of judgment at that time was a severe drought, and God called Elijah to be his messenger of this news. Elijah announced the calamity as expected, and after his obedience, God told Elijah that he had to leave his "here" and go to a "there" in order for his needs to be met. Elijah needed food and water and couldn't find it "here" (due to the drought) so he had to leave and go to God's chosen "there" to receive it. Once Elijah obeyed and moved to where God wanted him, it was *only then* that God supernaturally instructed birds to bring him food while Elijah was placed alongside a brook as a water supply. This concept of leaving "here" to go to "there" could be argued as God's "Here-There Principle."

We must understand that when God calls us to leave our current circumstances, it is because he plans to bless us once we get to the "there" in our lives. The journey may be (and usually is) difficult. That journey may not even make sense to us at the time. We may not even know the reason(s) he wants us to move, but when he guides us through his spirit, we should follow. This is not only a test of our obedience and devotion to him, but it is also a means for us to better learn just how much God loves us. Furthermore, it is how we learn to rely on God for everything we need even when it requires supernatural miracles to happen. This of course strengthens our faith, and as our faith grows, so too will our confidence that following God's leading is exactly what we need to be doing. It works cyclically.

For a few other Biblical examples of the "Here-There Principle" being put into effect, consider Genesis 12:1-4. God told Abram to "leave your country... and go to the land I show you." Then God promised Abram that his seed would be made into a great nation and be blessed. God's will for Abram was that he receive his blessing in a foreign country. Abram could only be blessed when he left his "here" and went to his "there." Also consider Ruth 1:1-7. We learn that Naomi was from Judah yet was living in another country (Moab) in verse one. Later, in verse six, we find that God was providing aid for his people (the

Jews) in their homeland while another drought was occurring throughout the Middle East. Naomi was "here" in Moab, yet God's blessings were "there" in Judah. The latter half of verse six declares, "Naomi and her daughters-in-law prepared to return home *from* (Moab)" – their "here" – and go "back to the land of Judah" – another "there." Due to Ruth and Naomi's faithfulness to God's call to move, the world would later receive the grandest blessing of all...the birth, death and resurrection of Jesus Christ. How so? We discover from a further reading of the Bible that Ruth met Boaz, married him, and was blessed with a child. This child became the grandfather of King David from whose lineage Jesus Christ came. Without Naomi's and Ruth's going from "here" to "there," there would be no Jesus. Lastly, consider Acts chapter nine, which concerns Saul's conversion. Saul was persecuting Christians to the point of death. On a road outside the city of Damascus, the resurrected Jesus himself met Saul, blinded him, and told him to "get up and go into the city." This is yet one more example of Jesus instructing a person (in this case Saul) to leave his "here" and go to a "there." Saul did so and because he went where God told him to go, Saul supernaturally received back his sight and was filled with the Holy Spirit. Saul could not have received his blessings had he stayed where he was because Jesus used Ananias as a vessel to miraculously return sight back to Saul.

Just as Elijah, Abram, Ruth, and Saul all received their blessings by moving from where they were at in life to another place God called them to be, I too was blessed by the Lord because I left my "here" back in 2003. However, I am no more favored in God's eyes than any other person, so we *all* can benefit from the "Here-There Principle" if we just obey God's directing. Once we learn what his will is for our lives, we have to then obey that instruction. Failure to do so could possibly result in us missing out on blessings. Additionally, obeying God also results in a satisfaction that is immeasurable since he promises us that his "waters (springs of life in a drought) do not fail."[176] An added benefit is that we also become closer to God throughout this entire process.

When God calls you to move out of a particular attitude or mind-set, he is instructing you to move from a "here" to a "there." When God calls you out of one profession into another, he is guiding you from a "here" to a "there." When God goes as far as telling you to move out of one state or your own

---

176 Isaiah 58:11; https://www.biblehub.com/isaiah/58-11.htm

country into another, he is literally asking you to move from "here" to "there." All three of these examples are difficult to consider, yet all three are wrapped in promises of blessing and the peace of knowing you are in God's will. How many times have you prayed that God make his will for your life clear? The key to gaining this clarity may rest in where God has been trying to move you.

FINITE OBSTACLES

Lack of trust in God's direction, Hesitancy to obey God when you know what he has asked of you, Stagnation

INFINITE TRUTH

God loves us enough to communicate his will to us. God also loves us enough to assure us that he will never leave us or forsake us, to walk with us through the valley of the shadow of death, and to bless our obedience. Knowing these truths, we shouldn't hesitate when God calls us to move from a "here" to a "there."

PRAYER

Heavenly Father, thank you for your guidance and instruction. Thank you for the wise concept of the "Here-There Principle" that can be seen throughout your Word. Please enable us to hear your voice when you call us to move from a here to a there and give us the ability to obey you when that call arrives. Forgive us for our failure to change when you require it. May our lives be altered to exalt you. In the name of Jesus, amen.

Lesson 21

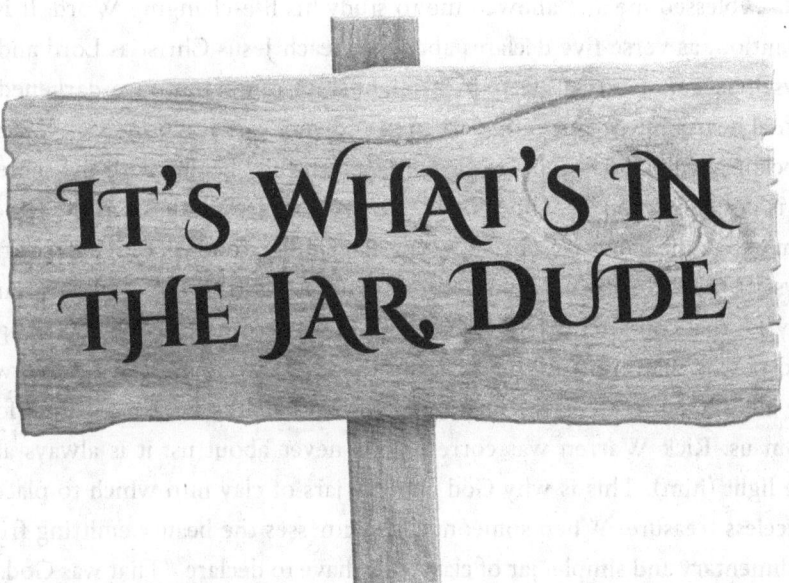

"For we do not preach ourselves, but Jesus Christ as Lord, and ourselves as your servants for Jesus' sake. For God, who said, 'Let light shine out of darkness,' made his light shine in our hearts to give us the light of the knowledge of the glory of God in the face of Christ. But we have this treasure in jars of clay to show that this all-surpassing power is from God and not from us. We are hard pressed on every side, but not crushed; perplexed, but not in despair; persecuted, but not abandoned; struck down, but not destroyed. We always carry around in our body the death of Jesus, so that the life of Jesus may also be revealed in our body. For we who are alive are always being given over to death for Jesus' sake, so that his life may be revealed in our mortal body. So then, death is at work in us, but life is at work in you."

II CORINTHIANS 4:5-12

Ever since I felt the Lord leading me to write this book, it has been my attempt to draw attention not to myself but to the Lord who has blessed me and allowed me to study his life-changing Word. It is my intention, as verse five declares above, to teach Jesus Christ as Lord and not myself because God calls us to let his light shine out of our once-darkened and carnal hearts into a currently darkened and very carnal world. Rick Warren's blockbuster book *The Purpose Driven Life* rightfully begins with the sentence, "It is not about you."[177] The apostle Paul truly understood this as the Lord led him to pen the above canonized words. Paul understood (as I am ever-learning myself) that we are just common earthen vessels (the Bible calls us "jars of clay")[178] that contain the truth of God when we become saved. It is God's glory and power that are truly the blessing that we and others can receive when we allow God to work through our lives so that "the light may shine forth" from us. Rick Warren was correct. It is never about us; it is always about the light (him). This is why God chooses jars of clay into which to place his priceless treasure. When someone else witnesses the beauty emitting from a rudimentary and simple "jar of clay," they have to declare, "That was God."

Matthew 5:2-12 records Jesus' very famous Sermon on the Mount. Also known as "the beatitudes," Christ taught a large crowd about who is truly blessed in life and exactly what real blessings truly are. Many of his statements seem contradictory when viewed through a worldly lens, but upon careful study, one will find that Jesus clarifies what a blessing is and how a blessing should be viewed. Many of us think a person is blessed by what they have. Of course we should thank the Lord for our possessions, but those "things" that will one-day pass away are not the true, permanent blessings of life. The true blessing for humanity is the eternal and abundant life that Jesus gives us when we place our lives in his hands and become saved. Jesus called this "living water."[179] This is because Christ lives eternally so the source of eternal life will never be extinguished.[180] We are also informed that from out of that person's heart will flow this same living water,[181] so part of that blessing is the truth that flows out of us to others as well. Lastly, this eternal blessing is a free gift once we come to Christ.[182]

---

177 *The Purpose Driven Life*, Rick Warren; 2002; p. 17.
178 Cf. II Corinthians 4:7
179 Cf. John 4:10-14
180 Cf. John 8:58; Colossians 1:17; Revelation 1:8 & 17
181 Cf. John 7:38
182 Cf. Revelation 21:6 with 22:17

The blessings that we receive that are discussed in the beatitudes are what shape us into joyous followers of Christ no matter our worldly circumstances. We can be earthly poor and still be greatly blessed. We can have few possessions yet we know we have been given *every* spiritual gift[183] at our second birth. We can be (and often are) persecuted, oppressed, ill, and crushed but we are assured that we are still filled with blessings from heaven for we know "life is always at work in us."[184] Even though the Lord allows us to go through trials and hardships in life, he still blesses his followers and it is often times *through* those trials rather than around them. He allows us to go through some terrible circumstances in life so that we can comfort and bless others who go through similar situations,[185] and when this occurs, we do not receive the glory. Instead, God receives the glory and that is how God has designed life. God will allow hardships in our lives to keep us humble servants of him, which frees him up to bless us because our pride no longer hinders his work. That is why Christ declared, "Blessed are the poor in spirit..." Pride and personal dependence are crushed when this occurs, which is truly a blessing.

A quick review of the other beatitudes reveals further blessings that shape us to be more like the character of Christ. We are blessed when we mourn (such as when I lost my son), which drives out the worldly value of finding happiness at any cost. We must not "sell our soul" for happiness; instead, we should allow God to transform us into creatures of joy no matter the circumstances. Those who are meek are blessed because they acknowledge God as the source of their power instead of themselves. Blessed are those who seek righteousness because we no longer pursue personal needs and instead allow God to supply them for us. Merciful people are blessed because it keeps them in touch with their feelings since mercy is an outflow of the Holy Spirit. It also yields compassion for our fellow man. The pure in heart are excellent candidates for leadership positions because the use of deception and threat of bribery are deemed unacceptable. The peacemaker is truly blessed, for that person finds that the world's chaos does not affect their own personal peace. And lastly, blessed are the persecuted because it strengthens their commitment to God.[186]

---

[183] I Corinthians 1:4-7; https://www.biblegateway.com/passage/?search=i+corinthians+1%3A4-7&version=NIV
[184] II Corinthians 4:8-12; https://www.biblegateway.com/passage/?search=2%20Corinthians%204:8-12&version=NIV
[185] Cf. II Corinthians 1:3-5
[186] For a solid, biblically-based argument on this topic, see the Internet article, "How Persecution Grows the Church" written by Pastor Jack Wellman at https://www.whatchristianswanttoknow.com/how-persecution-grows-the-church/.

We are eternally blessed not by what we have but because of who we are in Christ, and once we come to Christ – the river of water that gives every good gift[187] – we can then begin to experience the true blessings captured in the parable of the beatitudes. It is God who places these treasures in us, and due to this, it is also God who receives the glory. While God is receiving his due glory, and because of his loving nature, we also benefit at the same time even if it appears to the world that we are "hard pressed" and "given over to death." "How so?" you might ask. The answer is because through these trials, we also become blessings to others suffering similar circumstances. As we affect others in a positive manner due to having gone through struggles similar to theirs, those people also recognize that God is due the glory as he supports them through us. This is a true depiction of what it means to be part of the body of Christ.

We must never lose sight of the fact that we are indeed ordinary jars of clay, but it is what is inside those plain jars that is the true blessing. If we are able to put down our pride and arrive at this understanding, it is then that the top of our jars are opened and can be filled with all of the treasures God wants to give us. This then enables us to pour out what is placed inside us when someone else is in need as God introduces them into our sphere of influence. That person then, when they see how truly blessed a messed-up person like ourselves can be, can say nothing other than "That had to be God!"

FINITE OBSTACLES

Pretension, Pomposity, Overestimation of our own strength, Failure to acknowledge Christ as King

INFINITE TRUTH

Christ is the Alpha and the Omega, and it is his "water of life" that strengthens us to be able to let his light shine out of us and for his glory.

---

187 Cf. James 1:17

PRAYER

Lord Jesus, the truths that flow from your Word are only eclipsed by you. We recognize that you are undeniably the life that fills our vessel. We humble ourselves before you so that your blessings may flow into our lives and then out of our lives to benefit others. Please forgive us of the times we failed to recognize your headship and strengthen us to be willing jars of clay for your good use. In your name, amen.

Lesson 22

Are You Barnabas, Paul or Timothy? The Answer is "Yes."

"Then Jesus went with his disciples to a place called Gethsemane, and he said to them, 'Sit here while I go over there and pray.' He took Peter and the two sons of Zebedee along with him, and he began to be sorrowful and troubled. Then he said to them, 'My soul is overwhelmed with sorrow to the point of death. Stay here and keep watch with me.' Going a little farther, he fell with his face to the ground and prayed, 'My Father, if it is possible, may this cup be taken from me. Yet not as I will, but as you will.' Then he returned to his disciples and found them sleeping. 'Could you men not keep watch with me for one hour?' he asked Peter."

MATTHEW 26:36-40

There was a time in my life where I faced an onslaught of troubles that occurred in a very short period of time. As I was a teacher in those days, my daily routine was attempting to motivate freshmen in high school to learn history. For those of you who teach or those of you with fourteen and fifteen year-old children, you can attest that this one responsibility is tough by itself. At the same time those daily stressors occurred, Renee and I had someone we trusted break into our house, which resulted in dissonance between the two of us as well as a set of new locks. I also coached baseball and had the difficult job of cutting players, so I also faced the numerous debates put forth from the parents of the players I cut in defense of their son's (often unrealistic) abilities. Those conversations are never easy. My father was also going through a divorce, suffering through similar assailments that many people experience in these terrible events, and watching it was like reliving a time I would rather forget. My sisters and I had to help my father move his stuff out of his house at the same time Renee and I were also moving into our own new home. I was thus faced with the time-sensitive task of readying our old house, packing, moving our stuff, and all of the financial responsibilities that come with home-buying while at the same time assisting my father with his move. I also learned at that time that my grandfather, who had been a rock in my life, chose to retire out of the ministry for health reasons, which led me to recognize my own sense of mortality more than I previously had. Thankfully, no one ever came to crucify me unjustly as happened to Jesus, but during that period of intense stress, I felt like "my soul (was) overwhelmed... to the point of death."

When I look back at that time that now seems less distressing than I remember when I was going through it, I recall taking an hour or so one evening to clear my thoughts of the seemingly overwhelming burdens I was experiencing. Instead of fretting my situation, I followed the apostle Peter's advice[188] and "cast my anxieties on God" by reading some psalms written by a king who underwent severe stress. While King David gave us a record of him pouring out his heart to God when he suffered, these psalms did not have the supporting effect I had hoped they would. I also remember praying extensive prayers of sincerity to the Lord. While I knew that the Lord always hears the

---

[188] I Peter 5:6-7; https://www.biblegateway.com/passage/?search=1+Peter+5%3A6-7&version=ESV

prayers of his children,[189] I didn't quite hear the answers I thought I needed. Perhaps you have also gone through a time, or maybe you are currently going through a time where the pressures of life are also overwhelming you. God does want us to cast our cares upon him as I did, but the response to my "casting" was not what I expected. I thought God would simply "give" me something internally to overcome the stress. The only thing he gave me at that time was a dose of his Word from Matthew chapter twenty-six.

In this chapter of Matthew, we find Jesus preparing to bear the burden of humanity's sins on his shoulders, and that was so weighty that it caused him to sweat blood![190] He knew he was about to be humiliated, tortured, and horrifically executed yet he demonstrated to us what we should do when we also become overwhelmed. Since he was the God-man who loved and healed so many, it is likely he had multitudes of people who would have prayed with him had he asked them to, but of the twelve men to whom he was closest, he only chose three of them for support while he was praying in the Garden of Gethsemane. Why? Since Jesus is God, couldn't he have simply prayed by himself and headed to the cross without this event having to be recorded? The answer is "Of course he could have," but instead, he set for us an example how to handle difficult situations. Like Jesus, we too need to seek out some trusted friends and pray.

Proverbs 17:17 declares, "A friend loves at all times, and a brother is born for adversity." Jesus understood that his friends – even though they would betray him for a short time – loved him even unto martyrdom. Instead of relying on God the Father to "give" him something to overcome his stress, Jesus understood the importance and truth of Proverbs 17:17. Christ knew he had brothers in faith who were born for adversity, and when this adversity arose, he leaned on these brothers. Based on this understanding, we too need to cultivate some friendships in life with a few close friends where the love-bond is so strong that we can pour out our spirit to them when we face inevitable times of trouble.

For some people, our families were born for these times. My sisters have been rocks in my life ever since we became adults. However, I also have needed fellow men in my life with whom I can share "man-stuff." God has brought

---

189 Cf. Proverbs 15:29
190 Luke 22:44; https://biblehub.com/luke/22-44.htm

me into contact with two such men over the years. One was named Don, but our relationship has unfortunately waned since I now live about 700 miles away from him. However, the Lord has now introduced me to a young man named Danny, and he and I have formed a bond of trust. One of the interesting dynamics that developed with these two men coincided with both my age and walk with Christ. I was in my early twenties when I became friends with a middle-aged preacher named Don. During this period of time, I was also a newer Christian and God used Don to not only be a "brother born for adversity," he also served as a mentor for my Christian journey. I miss Don and have pondered why that relationship sort of just faded away. I believe the answer is found in Job 17:9. We learn from this verse that despite what happens to us, we should always hold to our ways (keep moving forward) for in doing so we become "stronger and stronger." God used Don as an older male influence in my life, and the Lord used him to help set a young me "on my way." Once God got me to a place where I was stronger in my faith, God chose to move me. Over time, as I got older and stronger, God replaced Don with a young man, and I became the older mentor God is now using to assist with making Danny stronger. A similar Biblical example of this process can be seen with the apostle Paul working closely with Barnabas at the beginning of his ministry, and after Paul became stronger, Paul and Barnabas parted ways. Paul then became a mentor to a young Timothy. The common denominator in all of the above stories is that we need close friends in our Christian walks. Sometimes God allows those relationships to blossom and then fade away. Sometimes he uses those relationships to mentor us or for us to mentor someone else. In all of those relationships, God uses the body of Christ so that we can help each other in our life-journeys.

How about you? Do you have someone that is willing to sit down with you and pray for you when you are in need? Is there a person in your life who will simply read the Bible to you and express to you what they believe the Lord is speaking to them? Jesus demonstrated to us that we need to not only take time away from life to pour out our hearts to God but that we should also do so at times with loving friends. Proverbs 27:6 informs us that "wounds from a friend can be trusted..." and Proverbs 27:10 cautions us not to "forsake your friend and the friend of your father, and do not go to your brother's house when disaster strikes you – better a neighbor nearby than a brother far away." Let us take God's advice to heart. Allow Jesus' example in the garden to teach us that we *do* need to cultivate some close friendships. You may be the mentor or the mentee, but God has chosen to utilize relationships with other people to grow and support us. I thank the Lord for that, for I know I'm never on an island alone when I go through the hurricane winds of life!

FINITE OBSTACLES

The belief that we can effectively make it through life on our own. A lack of friends and/or family or an unfortunate situation where friends and/or family are not as trustworthy as we would like.

INFINITE TRUTH

Jesus is a friend who will never leave us or forsake us regardless of what we do, say, or think. He loves us enough that if we ask him for sound Christian friends, he will make the divine appointments necessary so that we come into contact with those people.

PRAYER

My prayer is that of Ecclesiastes 4:9-12: Dear Lord, you inform us that "Two are better than one, because they have a good return for their work: If one falls down, his friend can help him up. But pity the man who falls and has no one to help him up! Also, if two lie down together, they will keep warm. But how can one keep warm alone? Though one may be overpowered, two can defend themselves. A cord of three strands is not quickly broken." May the Lord bless you today as you tackle the trials of life, and may he bring into your lives people with whom you may fellowship to the glory and honor of Christ.

Lesson 23

No Reserves, Retreat, or Regrets

"What does it profit, my brethren, if someone says he has faith but does not have works? Can faith save him? If a brother or sister is naked and destitute of daily food, and one of you says to them, 'Depart in peace, be warmed and filled,' but you do not give them the things which are needed for the body, what does it profit? Thus also faith by itself, if it does not have works, is dead. But someone will say, 'You have faith, and I have works.' Show me your faith without your works, and I will show you my faith by my works.

JAMES 2:14-18

I was exposed to the biography of William Whiting Borden[191] one morning, and the first thing I thought of after reading it was how his actions exemplified the spirit of what James conveys to Christians in his epistle. The above verses in the book of James have often been a reference for people declaring that the Bible contradicts itself, especially when these verses are juxtaposed with Ephesians 2:8-9. However, a deeper study into the instruction of both Paul and James reveals they are not in conflict, and a penetrating study of Borden reveals he understood the teachings of both early Church fathers. Paul's guidance is correcting an error of legalism[192] while James is correcting an error of antinomianism.[193] Paul's target audience is the sinner, a label of which Borden obviously considered himself when he gave his life to Christ. James targets the already-saved, which Borden professed to be and his actions further revealed.

Borden was heir to a fortune back at the turn of the 20th century, and he was already a millionaire by the time he graduated high school at the age of sixteen. When he enrolled at Yale University, he was such a devout follower of Jesus that some of his classmates at Yale later went on record stating that he was a stalwart regarding his walk of faith with the Lord. What an incredible compliment. As Borden grew older and closer to the Lord, he felt a call to missionary work. In what cannot be considered anything but providential leading, he believed retaining his fortune would keep him from relying on God. He understood his own sin-nature better than many Christians, for he knew he would have the tendency to rely on his wealth when times would inevitably get tough while on his missions. Stunningly, Borden declined his entire fortune in his early twenties and it is alleged that in his Bible he wrote the words "No Reserves."

After his days at Yale, Borden graduated from Princeton Seminary and upon completion of his graduate work, he sought to witness to the Muslim people of

---

191 For brief biographies of William Borden and timelines related to him, see articles that can be found at http://yalestandard.com/biographies/borden-of-yale/ by *The Yale Standard*, https://www.moodymedia.org/articles/william-whiting-borden/ by Beulah Bishop, and https://www.classicchicagomagazine.com/near-sainthood/ by Megan McKinney.

192 To gain a deeper understanding of scriptural legalism, Dr. Stephen J. Nichols wrote an article for Ligonier Ministries entitled "The Roots of Legalism" that does well explaining how grace is the only thing that prevents sinful man from looking inwardly and thus falling into the error of legalism. This article can be read here: https://www.ligonier.org/learn/articles/roots-legalism/.

193 Two Ligonier Ministry articles that do a good job helping the reader understand antinomianism are "The Antinomian Error" by R.C. Sproul, which can be found here: https://www.ligonier.org/learn/devotionals/that-antinomian-error/ and "The Antinomian Way of Justification" by John Gerstner found here: https://www.ligonier.org/blog/antinomian-way-justification/.

China known as the Uyghurs. Borden realized that he needed to learn Arabic to better communicate with them so he went to Egypt to develop his language skills. While he was in Egypt, Borden caught spinal meningitis and became very ill. While fighting the effects of this debilitating disease, Borden refused the almost inevitable temptation to simply give up his calling and return home to the family fortune. In a demonstration of his devotion to God's call on his life, Borden is also alleged to have written in his Bible the words "No Retreat."

One month after arriving in Egypt, Borden lay ill on what would become his death bed. As he prayed and sought the Lord for comfort, he must have been reviewing his life up to that point. He was a bright, twenty-five-year-old young man who had one of the premiere last names in Chicago. He was rich. He began a successful campus ministry at Yale University and had become the director for the Moody Bible Institute at the tender age of twenty-two. He had what many people would have considered a "great life," yet he gave it all away to serve Jesus. Shortly before Borden died a month after arriving in Cairo, he allegedly again wrote in his Bible the words "No Regrets" underneath his previous two entries.

William Borden understood profit according to both man's and God's economies. His short yet impressive life reveals that he was much more interested in profiting from God than he was from men. He knew there were many people who were spiritually "destitute" and "naked" in their sinfulness, and if he turned a deaf ear to them to live out what men call "the good life," his faith in Christ was of little value. Borden made a decision early in his life that he was going to show everyone his faith by his works. While he did not ultimately accomplish his goal of witnessing to the Uyghurs, Borden's epitaph appropriately described his short life with the concluding statement: "Apart from faith in Christ, there is no explanation of such a life."[194]

When one evaluates his famous six-word quote of "No Reserves; No Retreat; No Regrets," it becomes apparent that Borden's unswerving devotion to the Lord would be seen by others through his "works" done unto Christ. As Borden eagerly awaited his Savior, he "worked" not *for* his salvation but *because* his "citizenship was in heaven."[195] He understood that his status in life, his wealth, and his name were nothing compared to the riches of Jesus,

---

194 See: https://www.findagrave.com/memorial/15641525/william-whiting-borden
195 Philippians 3:20; https://www.biblehub.com/philippians/3-20.htm

and he further understood that his efforts would be a visible instrument of righteousness.[196] He touched thousands of lives while alive, and, even as you read this, he is still touching lives today for you are learning of his devotion to Christ over one hundred years later.

Both the apostle Paul and James the brother of Jesus discussed "works" in their writings, but each of them was addressing a certain aspect of works. Borden understood that Paul's "works" were efforts a sinner attempts in order to earn his salvation. In what can be described as a salvation by works, this is the legalism of which Paul rejected. Borden also understood that once he was saved by God's grace alone, his faith in Christ would be made alive by the efforts he put forth as an instrument of righteousness. This can be described as the "works" to which James was referring. Borden was a man who understood theology. When studied in its entirety, we will discover that everything written in the Bible is harmonious and non-contradictory. We can all look back at the life of William Borden and see a perfect example of how a person – once saved – will demonstrate works for the Lord in an effort to be a living sacrifice[197] back to God for the grace he showed that person through the grace of salvation. If you haven't already accepted God's gracious gift of salvation, would you do so today? And if you already have received his free gift of salvation, consider what works are evident in your life that demonstrate the fact that you are saved?

FINITE OBSTACLES

Temporary treasures that will one-day pass to others when we die or pass away over time. A false sense of security based on anything that is not the Lord Jesus Christ.

INFINITE TRUTH

True security and wealth can only be found in a relationship with our Creator. This relationship is the one treasure all people have available to them but many unfortunately never accept.

---

196 Cf. Romans chapter six
197 Cf. Romans 12:1

PRAYER

Dear heavenly Father, we come to you humbly today with gratitude for your grace. You loved us so much that you sent your son to pay a penalty for sin that no person could ever pay regardless of the "works" they do. Because of your salvation, you have freed Christians to utilize the gifts of the Holy Spirit as tools we can use to work for your kingdom. It is these "works" that help define a person devoted to Christ, not a way a person comes to Christ. Please give us a spirit to fulfill your calling on our lives so that we may glorify you with what we do. In Christ's holy name, amen.

Lesson 24

So he said to me, "This is the word of the Lord to Zerubbabel: 'Not by might nor by power, but by my Spirit,' says the Lord Almighty."

ZECHARIAH 4:6

There are sometimes events in our lives that serve to reveal just how feeble we humans can be. When I was diagnosed with cancer, I experienced physical frailty. When Renee and I suffered through not one but two miscarriages, we both became familiar with the emotional pain of losing children. There was also a time in my life where Renee went through a horrific tragedy involving her best friend. It was during this period of grief that I realized no matter how much I love someone and desire to meet their needs, I really did not have the power to do so despite my best efforts. What I have done in this lesson was transcribe what I had written in real-time back in the year 2009 while those events were occurring. I have done this in an effort to capture the sincerity of what I was experiencing at that time. My goal is that this transcription illustrates the authentic struggle with which I was wrestling at the time. It was a tragic story, but at the end of this lesson, now that I am writing this book many years after the event, I will update the reader with what actually transpired. I trust the purity of this account will help drive home God's message to us all that only he truly has the power to meet our every need.

Last month, on a cool October weekend, Renee and I decided to head down to her original home of southern Illinois. She and I met two of her long-time friends so that the three ladies could catch up on old times. This was the first time I had ever met these two ladies who had been friends with Renee since she was in high school. In fact, one of them, Carla, had enough influence in Renee's earlier life that the two of them decided they would go to college together after high school. Carla and Renee were even roommates while they attended school and became the closest of friends as a result. Rather tragically, my first opportunity to meet and converse with Carla in October was also my last. Carla was unfortunately in a car accident the following January and as a result probably will pass away at the young age of thirty-eight.

For the past week I have observed the deep sorrow that has affected Renee as a result of this tragedy. I have done my best to be supportive and understanding of Renee, and on a few occasions I have been unable to find the right words to say and therefore chose not to say a word at all. I have in effect once again encountered my humanity. I have realized through this painful time for my wife and difficult time for me that I am unable to fulfill the deepest needs of my wife. I have become aware that only the power of the Lord himself is able to keep us when times are tough.

This feeling of feebleness is probably not unlike that felt by Mary Magdalene and Mary the mother of Jesus when they visited Jesus' tomb. Matthew 28:1-10 is one account of the interaction between these two women and an angel of the Lord. This was the angel who had rolled back the stone blocking Christ's tomb, and he was sitting on it when the two Marys showed up. He told them that Jesus was not in the tomb; that he was risen just as the Lord said would occur. He then instructed the two Marys to go tell Jesus' disciples of the news. Verse eight declares, "So the *women hurried away from the tomb, <u>afraid</u> yet filled with joy, and ran and told his disciples" (emphasis mine).*

The two Marys were in a situation similar to that which Renee and I are in. Both were very aware of their frailty and humanity during a time of personal loss, and they were afraid. Fear is a gripping emotion that is not of the Lord. It is very real and can render a human powerless in a matter of seconds. However, the prophet Zechariah tells us that it is not by our power that we can do anything anyway. We cannot overcome fear on our own. We cannot make it through tragic life-experiences by our own strength. We cannot do anything apart from the power and strength of the Holy Spirit of God.

Consider David when he faced Goliath: It was not the slingshot that empowered the feeble shepherd boy to face and defeat the redoubtable Philistine; it was the power of the Lord. Consider Moses. Three times he tried to talk God out of sending him before the most powerful man on the earth at that time, Egypt's pharaoh. Yet, through the power of God, Moses was used to rescue the Hebrews out of Egypt. Consider Gideon. When approached by the angel of the Lord and called "mighty warrior" by God, he argued with the angel declaring that he was the youngest son in the weakest family of a mediocre tribe of Israel and that he could not possibly be the one to defeat the enemies of God. He crushed the Midianites but not of his own strength. No, it was the power of God.

When God allows painful, even fearful events to occur in our lives, we must remember that God has promised his children the power of his Holy Spirit. It is the same Spirit that had the power to raise up Jesus from the dead even though he bore every single sin of humanity on his shoulders. It is the same power that parted the Red Sea. It is the same power that saved you and I from our own sins, and it is the same power that can strengthen us when we tragically lose a loved one. Do not be fearful of tapping into the power afforded us through the grace of God. Rely not on our human feebleness and lean instead upon the strong hand of God. Only through his might and power can we face the hard times experienced on earth. Only through his might and power can we find good when the devil will tell you all is lost.

That concludes what I had written back in 2009, but I am now honored to be able to tell the rest of the story. Carla was in a coma for many weeks. Her family spent much time by her bedside, but the doctors finally informed them that she would never again leave the hospital. Carla's family had made the excruciating decision to unplug her life support equipment, but before doing so, everyone got a chance to say their last "goodbyes." Each one of them took turns making their peace while fighting through heavy tears and pain. Eventually, both of Carla's nieces came and sat on her bed to make their peace. When that occurred, Carla's eyelids began to flicker. Since this had been the first movement of any kind expressed by Carla since the accident, the staff were notified immediately. They began to check her life-support machines, and they apparently showed something encouraging. Based on the small eye movements Carla was showing, the family decided not to take her off of her life-support machines at that time.

In what can be attributed to nothing short of an act of God generated by the very power of the Holy Spirit of which I reference above, Carla eventually awoke from her coma. After undergoing months of therapy, she now lives with her mother, volunteers at the local hospital consoling accident victims, and has been to our house a number of times. She is literally a walking miracle. She has shared with us that when doctors scan her brain and review the images, they tell her every time that what they see on film does not correlate with a walking, talking woman. Carla always gives credit to God for this, and she has been given a story that makes for a great testimony of the power of the Holy Spirit. To her credit, she tells that story and has given me permission to share it with you as well. Renee and I are so happy to see that God has used her best friend to touch others who are suffering through tragedies that reveal our human frailties can only be overcome by the Lord Jesus.

FINITE OBSTACLES

Human feebleness, Human infirmities, Confusion, Sadness, Physical death

INFINITE TRUTH

God has omnipotent power and has conquered even death itself. Once we accept Christ as our Lord and savior, we are then able to ask him to use that power in ours and other's lives for God's glory.

PRAYER

Dear Lord, thank you for your Word. Thank you that you have overcome this world, and thank you for even overcoming death. Thank you for imparting your power into our lives through the Holy Spirit. Please enable us to lean not on our own understanding and to instead place our trust and faith in you. Please comfort those of us suffering through painful experiences right now, and empower us to overcome the obstacles before us. In the powerful name of Jesus, amen.

LESSON 25

YOU HAVE TO DIE BEFORE YOU CAN LIVE

> "I tell you the truth, a grain of wheat must fall to the ground and die to make many seeds. But if it never dies, it remains only a single seed. Those who love their lives will lose them, but those who hate their lives in this world will keep true life forever. Whoever serves me must follow me. Then my servant will be with me everywhere I am. My Father will honor anyone who serves me."
>
> JOHN 12:24-26

Many of us who have been saved have stories that are similar. Our details vary, but the fact that we can identify a "before I was saved me" versus an "after I was saved me" is typical. I was an arrogant idolater, interested only in achieving greatness through the game of baseball when I was the "before I was saved me." I am thankful that I never got into drugs, but I did succumb to lust. I was addicted to tobacco, and I was once fairly mean-spirited, willing to say whatever came to my mind. A lot of people write off such actions as deriving from immaturity. I admit those are immature actions, but I will also argue with anyone who tries to attribute them solely to age-based immaturity. I will be the first to admit to you that my once-shameful actions were immature alright...I acted that way because I was *theologically* immature. What I mean by this is that I did not know Christ so I therefore did not know truth. I was following my sinful nature, and that nature sought to serve only "self." Perhaps you too have had a time where God brought you face-to-face with his Word, and it served as a mirror, reflecting back the ugliness that could be identified only as "me." I am thankful for that mirror-experience, for I realized that the man looking back at me in that mirror had to die. Not physically (yet), but that spiritual sin-nature had to go. Once I learned the truth of the gospel, I was able to put that "old me" in the grave, only to be resurrected a "new me" and unto the Lord Jesus Christ.

The words spoken in the above verses were uttered by Christ. He was (as verse twenty of the same chapter tells us) speaking to both Greeks and Jews, which establishes that his message of forgiveness and salvation is for anyone who would follow him. Additionally, a few lessons can be surmised from this passage as well. When Jesus uses this kernel of wheat illustration, he is demonstrating how we actually become more fruitful when we die to ourselves and give him all of the junk that we brought with us to God's kingdom when we were saved. When Jesus became Lord of our lives, he became Lord over all of our qualities and good points as well as all of our vices and junk. Verse twenty-five explains to us that we have to die to ourselves – our own selfish desires...what we want...holding on to the sins of our past...the hurts and pains we've experienced...the anger, bitterness and resentments we have toward others and ourselves...the plans we have for our own lives and careers – *all* of it must be given to God. This is not easy to do, yet the singular wheat kernel "dies" when planted but is later harvested as a new stalk of valuable wheat bearing many more seeds for food or future harvests. In this parable, Jesus shares with us one of many paradoxes that can be found in scripture: We have to die in order to live, and he personally demonstrated to us that he is in fact correct. He came to earth in order to die, yet by dying he not only resurrected himself and lives as crowned King over everything, he also gives us the opportunity to live as royal children of God if we only accept his gracious payment for our sins and follow him.

This brings us to verse twenty-six, which declares that we "must follow him if we are to serve him." What does Jesus mean by "follow him?" In order to understand this, just continue studying the gospel records. He went to his death physically and also spiritually. We read in Luke 22:39-46 that Jesus went to the Garden of Gethsemane and asked God the Father to "...take this cup from me; yet not my will, but yours be done." Jesus knew he would not only suffer the physical torture of Roman crucifixion but that he would also bear the terrible spiritual burden of all of mankind's' sins as well as be separated from the Father. But because he loved us so much, he still carried out what he was born to do, which is dying and resurrecting so that we could come into communion and right-standing with God by grace alone. Jesus' command to "follow him" requires us to do the same. We must allow the Lord to crucify our selfish desires and resurrect us to a new, abundant life in Jesus Christ. The wheat must be planted and die in order to sprout up as a new vibrant stalk of useful wheat that bears many more seeds to be planted in the future. We too must lay down what we want for our own lives so that Christ can replace it with his will for us. This is how we follow Christ. We follow his example of self-sacrifice to fulfill God's will.

Lastly, Jesus gives us the promise that, "My Father will honor the one who serves me." This gift of reassurance should gracefully empower us to do what is sometimes incredibly hard – giving up our desire to control our life and allowing God to call all the shots instead. As mentioned above, Jesus is Lord of both the good parts of your life and the bad parts of your life as well, and we should actually thank God for that! God does not leave us where we are.[198] He does know about your pains and hurts.[199] He knows what happened to you in your past. Romans 8:28 explains to us that God takes all of the things that occurred to us in our past, even the events that were not of his will nor caused by him, and he will work them for good in the lives of his children. This means any sexual abuse you may have suffered; any mistreatment and pain caused by a former or current spouse; any emotional and/or physical abuse you may have

---

[198] Cf. Deuteronomy 31:6 & 8; I Chronicles 28:20; Joshua 1:9; Matthew 28:20; I John 1:9; Psalm 55:22
[199] Cf. Psalm 56:8

suffered from a stranger or parent; any losses in life you may have suffered, and any and all tragic events that have ever occurred in your life are known by God[200] and he promises his children that he uses them for good. God does not say to us, "Get over it." He is not that rude. He loves us too much to say such a selfish and hurtful statement. Christ died on the cross and rose again so that you can get over it, whatever that may be.[201]

How can we apply this passage to our lives today? First we have to confess our sins and give our life to Christ.[202] We then need to forgive ourselves, our enemies, and those in our lives with whom we hold resentment. We cannot do this under our own power, which is why it takes the power of the Holy Spirit to accomplish.[203] Forgiveness really is a privilege that frees us to not only love others and ourselves but also gives us freedom to accept the grace and love afforded us by God.[204] We have to get out of "Prison Warden-mode" and get into "Forgiving Christian-mode" if we truly want to live a joyful life. Once we are saved and then truly and completely forgive ourselves and others, this gets us into the correct, humble position where God can begin being Lord of our junk and working it for good in our lives. The parable of the wheat is symbolic of what happens to us when we die to Christ. We are buried with him, and given a second nature[205] so that Christ can live through us. It is then that we, like the seed of wheat, can then bear much more fruit than was initially buried.[206]

Would you like to experience the release of guilt? How about the freedom of having forgiven your enemy so the bitterness you may be experiencing can be put down? Maybe being able to "get over" the pain you experienced as a child is what you seek. It can all be done by dying to Christ and allowing him to resurrect your life unto him and his will just as the wheat kernel perished in order to bring forth a harvest of new, fresh wheat stalks. Jesus does give abundant life but only after we give up our lives to him. Just as he died and rose again, so too may we, but only through him.[207]

---

200 CF. Psalm 139:1
201 For a review of what Christ's resurrection accomplished for us, see Bryan Jay's article "Because Jesus Rose from the Dead" at https://gospelforchristians.com/2009/matthew-281-6-because-jesus-rose-from-the-dead/.
202 Cf. I John 1:9
203 Cf. Ephesians 4:31-32; Acts 3:19; and Colossians 1:13-14
204 Cf. Ephesians 1:7
205 II Peter 1:4; https://www.biblehub.com/2_peter/1-4.htm
206 John 15:8; https://biblehub.com/john/15-8.htm
207 Cf. John 11:25

FINITE OBSTACLES

The results of sin, whether that be pain, anger, bitterness, fear, jealously, rebellion, or any other result of your sin or someone else's.

INFINITE TRUTH

Jesus came to die and then be resurrected so that you and I can take up his light burden rather than having to carry the impossible burden that resulted from sin. All we have to do is accept him as Lord and savior, and he will begin the lifelong process of reclamation and healing.

PRAYER

Dear Lord, thank you for the privilege of being able to give our lives to you and be forgiven of our own sins. Thank you for the gracious gift of being allowed a second, righteous nature that allows us to forgive and lead a blessed and eternal life. Thank you for the guidance you give us in your Word. Thank you for being Lord of all, and that includes our messed-up lives. Thank you for the promise to work all things for good to those called according to your purpose. Please touch our hearts today and empower us with the courage to die to ourselves so that we may live for Christ. Bless this act of faith and make our efforts fruitful for your kingdom. Allow us to experience the feelings of release from "Unforgiver's Prison" once we do this, and fill the void in our hearts with your love. In the name of Jesus, amen.

LESSON 26

"We will not neglect the house of God."

NEHEMIAH 10:39(B)

Early in our marriage, Renee and I were once greeted at our home by two unwelcomed guests. We were living in a small condominium, and the carpeting in our bedroom was beginning to gather upwards due to it having stretched over time. We hired a man to come in so that he could pull the carpet tight and cut off the excess that was causing the wrinkly fold to occur. Alongside one of our bedroom walls was the exterior wall to the entire condominium complex. In order to pull our carpet taut, our contractor had to remove a base board in order to tuck in the edge of the carpet. When he removed it, he noticed some black mold that had been growing behind the base board and was creeping onto and underneath our carpet. He asked me to come look at it, and when he grabbed the carpet and lifted it up so that we could see just how far the mold had crept, we both saw numerous pieces of what looked like "moving rice" under the carpet and drywall. It quickly became apparent that I had a much bigger problem than just a loose carpet: Mold and termites. Renee and I were ultimately displaced from our home while the necessary repairs could be made, the termites could be killed, and the mold could be evacuated from the home. While our home was small, the job was much bigger than either one of us anticipated. We were outside of our home for eighty-three days.

As that time away from home wound down, I was once sitting at my desk before school, reading the Bible and reflecting back on the previous two and a half months we spent temporarily living with my grandparents. The image of mold and termites was forever branded into my memory, and the idea that two unwelcomed guests were working day and night to destroy my home was on my mind. That morning, I had just finished reading chapter ten of the book of Nehemiah and the verse above simply jumped off of the pages at me. Renee and I had unknowingly neglected our home, which resulted in it being eaten away small bits at a time. Of course we did not intentionally seek to harm our home, but the damage occurred nonetheless. In a moment where the Holy Spirit used an immediate reality in my life to connect it with the wisdom of his Word, I realized that what had happened to me physically was also true for many of us spiritually. Even if we do not intend to neglect our walk with the Lord, many of us do, and it invites "unwelcomed guests" into our lives that operate behind the woodwork to damage what we value.

In Nehemiah, the Israelites had just made a promise to do all of the right things for God, but a study of their history reveals they were not able to keep up their end of the bargain because *all* of mankind is not able to do what the law requires. They intended to take care of God's house, but they did not. I too have had great intentions of doing what the Lord asks of me, but I too have neglected what I sought to do. The impact of this realization gave me a wrenching sort of feeling in my stomach, and I had one of those "gulping" moments. I was convicted by my study of Nehemiah chapter ten because even when I pledge to focus on God's calling (to not neglect the house of the Lord), I still do sometimes.

I Corinthians 6:19-20 inform us that our bodies are a temple of the Holy Spirit[208] and serve as a house of God. As I consider my own life, I recognize that I have neglected this "house" by my failure to live as I should. Indeed, there have been many times in the past that I should have done much more to help the cause of God's kingdom but I chose not to for what I likely believed at the time were good reasons. As I mature in Christ, I am realizing that the entirety of God's Great Commission[209] is rather simple. God asks us to witness for him to a lost world and when we do not live out our faith, we effectively neglect what God cares about most. God loves everyone on this planet, and he does not wish anyone to perish.[210] It is his will that everyone come to salvation, but we Christians often neglect the "house" (the church) that Christ is building. We tend to get caught up with pressures of this life and the concerns of the moment which results in us neglecting to carry out our commission. When we neglect God's "house," it allows the effects of sin to serve as unwelcomed guests that eat away at the blessings God intends for us and others.

Jesus gave us the formula for tending to his house in Matthew 22:36-40. When asked by a Pharisee, *"Teacher, which is the greatest commandment in the Law?" Jesus replied: 'Love the Lord your God with all your heart and with all your soul and with all your mind. This is the first and greatest commandment. And the second is like it: Love your neighbor as yourself. All the Law and the Prophets hang on these two commandments'."* When we love the Lord with our all, we will share the Gospel of Jesus Christ to those who are not Christians because we are forever grateful for his grace. When we understand that Christ loved us so much that he chose to die for us even though we were sinners,[211] we seek to live lives that glorify the Lord. Living righteous lives – ones conformed to the image of Christ[212] – is also a manner in which we glorify our Lord. Serving our fellow Christians is also a requirement as well to glorify God and give careful attention to his house. When we fail to speak the truth,[213] live out the truth, or withhold the compassion and lovingness of the truth, we in essence neglect the house of God.

---

208 https://www.biblegateway.com/passage/?search=1%20Corinthians%206:19-20&version=NIV
209 Cf. Matthew 28:16-20
210 II Peter 3:9; https://biblehub.com/2_peter/3-9.htm
211 Cf. Romans 5:8
212 Cf. Romans 8:29
213 Cf. John 14:6

Jesus did not focus on what an ordinary man wanted.[214] He instead focused on "not neglecting the house of God." He was not selfish. He didn't say, "You know, I don't feel like doing this or that today for God, so I am not going to." He didn't say, "I don't care what the other person wants. I want it my way and that's what I'm going to do." Jesus set the perfect example for us to emulate. If we seek to "not neglect the house of God," we need to witness to a lost world.[215] We do this not only by speaking truth, we also do so by stirring others to love and good works,[216] contributing to the needs of the saints,[217] fellowshipping in our homes,[218] walking in the light,[219] and doing good to all people.[220] This world is desperate for positivity, support, kindness, love, and forgiveness. The only way people can receive these gifts is for God's people to allow Christ to live out his life through us so that he can tend to his Father's house through us. The Lord tells us we are lights to the world like illuminated cities on a hill[221] where those walking in the dark valleys can look toward for shelter and safety. When we tend to people and their needs, we are acting in a manner that takes care of God's house.

Just as the Israelites fell into idolatry, we too live in the same fallen world that offers us lots of opportunities to neglect God. When a nation falls into idolatry, the people and the nation both lose their prosperity.[222] The United States and its people have lost much of our prosperity because we are guilty of neglecting God, and we need to repent and get back on the right track. Are you giving God the first portion of your time, your treasure, and your talents as he clearly lays out in Deuteronomy and again reiterates in Nehemiah? Or are you simply doing what most of us are guilty of and giving God what is left over, and that's if you have anything left over to give at all? As a teacher, I require my students to daily make conscious decisions concerning what they do with their time and talent. God is the "Great Teacher," and he requires no less.

I would argue that every one of us should reflect on our lives and consider where we neglect God. Once we identify those areas, we simply need to

---

214 Cf. John 5:30, 6:38 and 8:29
215 Mark 16:15-16; https://www.biblegateway.com/passage/?search=Mark%2016:15-16&version=NIV
216 Hebrews 10:24-25; https://www.biblegateway.com/passage/?search=Hebrews+10%3A24-25&version=ESV
217 Romans 12:10-13; https://www.biblegateway.com/passage/?search=Romans+12%3A10-13&version=ESV
218 Acts 2:42-47; https://www.biblegateway.com/passage/?search=Acts+2%3A42-47&version=ESV
219 I John 1:7; https://www.biblehub.com/1_john/1-7.htm
220 Galatians 6:10; https://www.biblehub.com/galatians/6-10.htm
221 Matthew 5:14; https://biblehub.com/matthew/5-14.htm
222 Cf. I Kings 11:1-11

repent and ask the Lord to help us remain cognizant of his commission. He is righteous. He is holy, and he demands that we be holy too. We can only do that through the power of the indwelling Holy Spirit and through the redemptive work of Jesus Christ. If you do not know the Lord but wish to, I invite you to pray the following simple prayer.

FINITE OBSTACLES

Self-indulgent debauchery, A false belief that we can do anything to earn righteousness, Failure to correctly discern scripture

INFINITE TRUTH

God gave us his Word, and in it are the instructions for all aspects of our life on earth. However, we have to first realize that we can never fulfill what is required of us (perfection) and come to a place of humility where we can admit this. Once we are at this place, it is then that we can give our lives over to Christ so that he can place us in his body of believers. Once we are in that body, it is then that we can begin taking care of God's house.

PRAYER

Dear Lord, I acknowledge that I have sinned against you as well as myself. I also admit that I cannot do anything to make myself right with you. Please forgive me of my sins; come into my heart and cleanse me of my unrighteousness. I no longer want to neglect you or your house, and I acknowledge that I can only do so with the power of the Holy Spirit. I invite you to be Lord of my life, and from this day forth I commit my life to you as your humble servant. In the name of Jesus, amen.

Lesson 27

Even Stormtroopers Cannot Break the Seal

> "When his master heard the story his wife told him, saying, 'This is how your slave treated me,' he burned with anger. Joseph's master took him and put him in prison, *the place where the king's prisoners were confined*" (emphasis the author's).
>
> · Genesis 39:19-20

One of my favorite series of movies has always been the George Lucas' *Star Wars* sagas. I especially find the first three to be classic Hollywood entertainment. While the theology revealed in this trilogy is definitely not Biblically-based, Lucas does include some scenes that can be used as familiar examples of how God acts on behalf of his children. In the seminal movie entitled *Star Wars: A New Hope*, there is a scene toward the beginning where the soldiers of the Dark Side, infamously known as "storm troopers," are looking to arrest the hero of the film, Luke Skywalker. He is traveling with his mentor Obi-won Kenobi to a cantina to look for a pilot. Both heroes get "pulled over" in a routine police check by several storm troopers. Since Kenobi was a full-fledged "Jedi master" (master of all things good in the movie series), he had learned a useful skill called the "Jedi mind trick."

What the mind trick did for the Jedi was enable him to transplant his thoughts into the minds of people whose minds were not as strong as his highly-developed and disciplined Jedi mind. In the scene, even though the storm troopers are looking right at the two men they are attempting to arrest, they do not realize it because Kenobi uses the Jedi mind trick on them. He simply tells the storm troopers that they are not in fact the two men they are looking for, and he also tells the lead storm trooper to let them "move along." Because Kenobi's mental will was theoretically stronger than the storm trooper's will, without hesitation, the storm trooper repeats the words implanted into his mind by Kenobi and the heroes dodge arrest. While I again repeat that the theology contained within the *Star Wars* movies is not an accurate reflection of Biblical principles, the idea that God has the ability to use something akin to a "Jedi mind trick" has some merit. God himself has given us a prime example of his ability to influence men's behaviors on earth, even to the point of making people do what he wants them to do as found in the verses above. God's ability to influence anything and everything whenever he wants is called "omnipotence."

In Biblical history, Joseph was a young, strong, and handsome man from Israel who was called by God to accomplish great things in ancient Egypt. His story can be found in Genesis chapters thirty-seven through thirty-nine. In sum, he was anointed by God but his older brothers became discontented with the way Joseph handled himself. Joseph was outspoken, and in a culture that placed lesser value on a younger sibling than an older one, this behavior didn't help matters between him and his older brothers. In time, his brothers plotted to kill Joseph. God first demonstrated his omnipotence by influencing the thinking of Joseph's brother named Judah. All of the brothers plotted to kill Joseph and cover up the murder but at the last second, the thought-processes of Joseph's brothers were obviously influenced by the Lord, for Judah recommended they change their plan. Ultimately, Joseph's life was spared and he was instead sold into slavery.

In an additional example of God being omnipotent and also working to shape the grand scenario of his will, God also used this time to shape Joseph, as he is again sold as a slave a second time once his original purchasers arrived in Egypt. While any number of Egyptians likely could have purchased Joseph upon his arrival, God's sovereignty is again apparent since the pharaoh's captain of the guard named Potiphar "happens" to be the one who purchases Joseph. Since God had a divine purpose for Joseph's life, God "was with him" and "gave him success in everything he did."[223] Due to his professional experience, it is apparent that Potiphar was a man skilled with being able to judge talent and character, and as a result, he decided to make Joseph the head of every aspect of the captain's estate. Effectively, a lowly slave anointed by God became second in command of Potiphar's household, second only to Potiphar himself. Genesis 39:5-6 tell us that the household of Potiphar was blessed because of the grace God showed Joseph.

One day Potiphar's wife sought to philander with Joseph and continued to make advances at him even though Joseph consistently refused and even avoided her. Eventually she was insulted by Joseph's refusal of her sexual advances and went to the point of grabbing him and commanding him to sleep with her. When he fled her unfaithful advance, he apparently ran out of his own coat, for he left his cloak in her grasp. Feeling scorned, she then turned on Joseph and made up a story that Joseph had attempted to rape her. When Potiphar's guards arrived to investigate the screams and saw Joseph's cloak in her grasp, her story became plausible.

In ancient Egypt as in 19th century America, slaves had little to no rights. Joseph was not an Egyptian, had no legal recourse against this false accusation, was owned by one of the most powerful men in Egypt, and was accused of attempting to rape this eminent man's wife. Furthermore, Potiphar's wife had evidence in her hands that what she declared was true. Now I ask you to put yourself in Potiphar's shoes. How would you have responded if you became aware of what seemed to be a clear-cut case of a slave trying to rape your wife? Everyone in Egypt knew that if Potiphar chose to kill Joseph, no one would question his action, and the thought of Potiphar simply arresting Joseph could be viewed as an extremely gracious if not unexpected response. It is likely that many men in Potiphar's situation would have at least entertained the thought

---

223 Cf. Genesis 39:3

of killing Joseph, and it can be reasonably expected that Potiphar would have wanted to as well. The verses above support this by sharing that Potiphar "burned with anger." However, we read in verse twenty that instead of reacting in an expected manner and killing Joseph, God may have played a "Godly mind trick" on Potiphar, for he instead placed Joseph in jail.

One of the many lessons that can be gleaned from this wonderful story is that when God has a purpose for your life (as he does for all of his children),[224] not even Satan himself can do things to divert God off of his will for your life. The prophet Isaiah informs us that "No weapon forged against (us) shall prosper,"[225] and Satan's plan to take Joseph's life was thwarted by a loving and sovereign God who would not allow his plans for Joseph, and by extension, the world to be altered. How awesome is it to know that we serve such a powerful and wise Lord?

To conclude this story, we discover that God later brought Joseph out of jail to oversee Egypt after the pharaoh appointed him as vizier, which made Joseph second in command of the entire Egyptian Empire. God further used Joseph to save the known world through a terrible drought, and he later became one of the patriarchs of Israel. Even if Satan puts out a contract on your life and intends to kill you by your siblings or by a plot of entrapment, God can and sometimes does foil those plans if he has a higher calling for your life. There are numerous stories of people who have survived incidents of danger when they should not have. Perhaps you are one of those people. God is sovereign, and it is because of his omnipotent hand that we are alive and prospering and we should recognize that and thank Jesus for his mercy. God has a purpose for every one of us, and he promises that he will see it through unto fulfillment. Seek his will. Get into the Word so that the Word gets in you. Pray. Allow the joy of knowing that as a Christian, you are sealed[226] by God and cannot be touched until God is through with your life. God's providence often works to enable you to serve him with determination. Thank him for his grace and sovereignty, for he has very likely already changed the minds of some Satanic storm troopers in your life's past and allowed you another day to fulfill his will for your life.

---

224 Cf. Romans 8:28
225 Isaiah 54:17; https://biblehub.com/isaiah/54-17.htm
226 Cf. Ephesian 4:30

FINITE OBSTACLES

Anything that is against the will of the omnipotent God

INFINITE TRUTH

God uses his sovereign providence to affect each person's life because he loves every one of us and does not wish any person to spiritually perish.

Prayer

Dear Lord, thank you for loving us enough that you sovereignly oversee our lives. Thank you that we can even learn lessons from a make-believe, pagan series of movies because you control everything. Please enable us to place you first in our lives and to do your will as desired. I ask these things in the name of Jesus, amen.

LESSON 28

> *"For this reason, since the day we heard about you, we have not stopped praying for you and asking God to fill you with the knowledge of his will through all spiritual wisdom and understanding. And we pray this in order that you may live a life worthy of the Lord and may please him in every way: bearing fruit in every good work, growing in the knowledge of God..."*
>
> COLOSSIANS 1:9-10

If you are a Christian, you are aware of the topic of prayer. Some of us view it as a concept that we don't fully understand; others regard it as something they do passively if the situation in their life dictates it.

Some pray only when going through tough times, seeking a sort-of "bail-out package" from the Lord. Still, others don't feel comfortable enough to do it at all. Lastly, there are some Christians who regard prayer as the only manner in which to remain plugged into their source of power, similar to the way an electrical appliance is powerless unless it is connected into an outlet.

Renee and I went to a "Weekend to Remember"[227] marriage conference one weekend, and out of all the information I learned in that short amount of time, the truth that struck me the hardest was a Biblical understanding of prayer. Sure, I acquired some excellent concepts and tools to be a better husband and father, but the most penetrating truth the Lord taught me that weekend was that I really cannot love God, my wife, or my children properly unless I pray, pray often, pray with them, pray for them, and lead by example in prayer as I ensure that we are a praying household. Upon review of my past prayer-life, I had to admit that I was not doing as well as the Lord expects me to and had to repent and ask for help to do better. Regardless of my past deficiencies, the experience in which Renee and I partook that weekend was based on God's truth and as a result, it was not just informational; it was transformational!

Before we become Christians, we acquired lots of knowledge, but the apostle Paul points out in verses nine and ten above that knowledge in itself is empty because it does not have the power to transform a person unto eternal life. A true knowledge of God is not empty because it results in a relationship with the living Christ and results in a changed life that yields spiritual fruit.[228] A quick review of the four books of the Gospel will reveal that Jesus' life modeled perpetual prayer. A further review of the Bible will indicate that God tends to use ordinary people to carry out his will, and he often chooses to do so through prayers.

Consider the prophet Nehemiah: He prayed all the time about everything he did and even before, through, and after he did what God called him to do. In fact, in the short book that bears his name, there are fourteen prayers recorded. Studying and reflecting on Nehemiah's prayers can serve as models to help us improve our own prayer lives. King David also prayed so much that God recorded many of his prayers in the book of Psalms. Moses had some of his prayers recorded in the Psalms too. Job prayed when times were good and

---

[227] For further information, see https://www.familylife.com/weekend-to-remember/
[228] Cf. Galatians 5:22-25

when times were awful in his life. The two primary evangelists of the initial church – Peter and Paul – were rock-solid prayer warriors, and many of their prayers can be read in multiple New Testament books. The list of both ordinary and extraordinary people praying in varying situations bespeckle the pages of the Bible to help create a beautiful mosaic of how we are to stay in touch with the true Vine[229] so that we continue to bear fruit for the kingdom. Thankfully, the Lord provides many examples of prayers for us in the scriptures that seem to indicate that people used of God, blessed of God, and committed to God are in fact praying people.

This begs the question...What really happens when we do pray? The Lord answers this for us through Paul's letter to the Colossians. One of the reasons we are to pray is because we do so as a method to bring our requests to God and specifically as a means to ask God to fill us with knowledge.[230] As a teacher, I have quickly ascertained just how feeble ignorance can make a person. Knowledge truly is power. God is omniscient (all-knowing), and that is one of the reasons he is the source of both truth and power. We too need Godly knowledge to be a strong tool for his use.

Secondly, prayer results in the bequeathing of spiritual wisdom and understanding to us from the Holy Spirit so that we may serve him in a pleasing way.[231] Jesus told us that we must remain in him for we can do nothing apart from him.[232] The only way we can "remain in him" is to commune with him through meditating on his Word, worshipping him, and praying regularly.[233] This is sound spiritual wisdom to consider when praying for your next major purchase, requesting healing from a sickness, or seeking guidance concerning how to deal with a rebellious child among many other things. Understanding God's Word because of the wisdom the Holy Spirit gives us from it assures us how to live as God requires. It further opens us up to the blessings afforded us through Christ and informs us how to apply God's truths to our lives so that we may live an abundant and victorious life through the inevitable trials we will face on this earth.

In addition to the knowledge, spiritual wisdom, and the understanding we can gain from prayer, we also gain instruction through the process of prayer since it is just one example of living a life that pleases the Lord. By praying,

---

229 Cf. John 15:5-8
230 Cf. Colossians 1:9
231 Cf. Colossians 1:9-12
232 John 15:4-6; https://www.biblegateway.com/passage/?search=John+15%3A4-6&version=NLT
233 Cf. Psalm 63:6, 1:2; Joshua 1:8; John 15:7, 14:13-14; I Thessalonians 5:17; Ephesians 6:18

we effectively are living a life that bears the fruit of good works. James 2:18 and verse 20 inform us that our professed faith in Christ is not of good use to the kingdom without us producing good deeds for the Lord. It is not by these deeds that we are saved, but it is honoring to the Lord and his kingdom when we commit good works as a response to the redemptive work that Christ did for us at Calvary. In essence, we are changed by Christ's saving grace and our response to him should be to live a life that serves him and seeks to honor his will. We know from references above that Christ does ask us to pray, and this is yet one way we obey him.

A fourth benefit of prayer is that it enables the Lord to develop endurance and patience in us. Renee and I have had our share of challenging events occur in our lives from being forced out of our home for three months shortly after being married due to the discovery of mold and termites, to the death of her parents, to her closest friend essentially dying from a car accident, to two miscarriages, to my battle with cancer and even more combat through the radiation treatments. You too can probably create a long list of struggles you have endured, and it seems that we learn patience best when we are forced through trials to rely on God's timing to work such tragedies out for our good. Communion with God through prayer then is a correct response that God desires when times in our lives are tough.

Young Christians must first learn to trust God's Word. As we mature in Christ, God takes our faith to a higher level by teaching us how to trust his silence. Learning to trust God's silence is a tough chore. If we can be empathetic with the Biblical characters of Joseph, Job, Mary and Martha the two sisters of Lazarus, we learn that we may be doing everything the right way but seeming to get the wrong results in this life. Remaining faithful to God during these times requires a lot of patience and endurance, but we can follow the judicious advice of Job during these times by continuing to hope in Christ[234] and accepting both bad and good results[235] because we know God is sovereign. We can also rest assured that as we learn through these trying moments and maintain our faith in God, he will reward those who seek him.[236]

A fifth component of prayer is that it affords us an opportunity to simply give thanks to God. Philippians 4:6 tells us that we are to combine thanksgiving

---

234 Job 13:15; https://biblehub.com/job/13-15.htm
235 Job 2:10; https://biblehub.com/job/2-10.htm
236 Cf. Hebrews 11:6

with prayer. In fact, the apostle Paul frequently introduced his letters with descriptions of how he thanked God for people when he prayed.[237] One of the reasons we should follow Paul's example is because prayer puts us in the right mindset to approach God. God made salvation available to an utterly evil mankind and for that we should be thankful. We should also be thankful that because of Christ's atonement,[238] we can now boldly approach the throne of God[239] in prayer. For this alone we should be thankful.

As you consider your walk with God during the coming week, reflect on your prayer life. Are you a person who views prayer as cumbersome? Do you reserve it solely for times of trouble, only during holidays, or specifically relegated to the dinner table? Are your prayers a laundry list of needs for God to fulfill, or do you approach prayer with a humble spirit and an understanding that it is your direct phone line to and from Jesus? I urge us all to reconsider our prayer lives, and just as I discovered at the aforementioned marriage retreat, a dedicated prayer life can bring us closer to God and our families while at the same time transforming our hearts into ones that are more devoted to serving our Lord Jesus.

FINITE OBSTACLES

Laziness and ignorance, especially when it concerns our prayer lives.

INFINITE TRUTH

Prayer is actually a blessing granted to humanity, and to take it for granted is to spurn a grand gift made available to us by the shed blood of Jesus Christ.

---

[237] Compare Romans 1:8; I Corinthians 1:4; Philippians 1:3-4; Colossians 1:3; I Thessalonians 1:2; II Thessalonians 1:3; II Timothy 1:3; and Philemon 1:4
[238] Cf. Matthew 27:50-51
[239] Cf. Hebrews 4:16

PRAYER

Heavenly Father, thank you for the wisdom and instruction of your Word. Thank you for illuminating the method of communication with you in your Word. Please forgive us for a complacent spirit, and teach us to come before your throne humbly and more consistently. In the name of Jesus, amen.

LESSON 29

GIVE GOD SOMETHING TO BLESS!

*"If you fully obey the LORD your God and carefully follow all his commands I give you today, the LORD your God will set you high above all the nations on earth. All these blessings will come upon you and accompany you **if** you obey the LORD your God."* (emphasis the author's).

DEUTERONOMY 28:1-2

Deuteronomy was one of the five books of the law written by Moses. Its contents seem to be an amalgam of history lessons, a briefing for future actions to be undertaken by God, a reiteration of God's covenant with humanity that he originally gave to Noah, and a government outline granted to the Israelites. This book is chocked full of lessons, but a primary theme running through chapter twenty-eight involves God informing his people numerous times that if they obey him, they will receive his blessings. On the contrary, if they disobey him, this will trigger many curses.[240] It is important to understand that this covenant was strictly for the Israelites. It was essentially a formal covenant by God to the Jewish people that outlines how God expected them to live with a declaration that a Messiah would come from their race to die on a cross for the sins of mankind. I do not want readers to misunderstand this lesson by thinking that God holds humanity to the Mosaic law today for salvation. This also does not mean that God has cast away his nation of Israel either. God still has a plan and love for Israel and will fulfill that plan completely in his timing.[241] This commitment that God established with the Jews is now identified as the "Old Covenant" because after Christ's death and resurrection, God established a "New Covenant"[242] for humanity that is based on grace.[243] While the Mosaic law lists many specific requirements[244] the Jews were expected to uphold, because this was exclusively for the Israelites in the pre-Christ era, both Jews and Gentiles now are no longer beholden to those specific requirements.[245] However, there are many universal moral obligations that are contained within the Old Covenant that still apply today because they are just that: universal. The Apostle Paul comments about Godly universal behaviors in Galatians 5:13, calling all Christians to use the freedom given them by Christ's grace to lovingly serve each other. We – like Paul – have to be diligent then to distinguish what commands are specific to the Old Testament covenant and which ones apply universally to both the Old and New Testament. In Christ, man is free, but he is not free to be lawless

One such universal obligation is the idea that God expects mankind to act in order to harvest a blessing. This has gone down in history as the principle of "reaping and sowing."[246] Jesus even references this principle in John 4:38. God does not want us to be complacent, expecting him to just open up the storehouses of heavenly blessings without committed action occurring. The

---

240 For an in-depth look at blessings and curses discussed with the nation of Israel, see Leviticus chapter 26; https://www.biblegateway.com/passage/?search=Hebrews+9%3A13-17&version=NASB1995
241 Cf. Psalm 105:8, 89:34; Jeremiah 31:31, 32:40; Leviticus 25:45
242 Cf. Matthew 26:28; Mark 14:24
243 Cf. Romans 9: 9-11; Hebrews 8:6-7, & 13; 9:13-17
244 For a list of the 613 laws given to the Jews, the writer(s) at Gospel Outreach Ministries Online break them down into positive and negative laws here: https://www.gospeloutreach.net/613laws.html
245 The Apostle Paul makes a comprehensive argument against "Judaizing" Christianity in the book of Galatians. The Jewish council in Jerusalem insisted that Gentile Christians must also uphold the Mosaic law (cf. Acts 15:5), and Paul wrote the letter to the Galatians to correct this error.
246 Cf. Galatians 6:7-9

Bible is clear that no man can work for his salvation[247] (which is indeed a blessing), and I do not want this lesson to be misunderstood as one that deceives people into thinking they can treat God as a sort-of vending machine that gives us what we want when we act a certain way. That is not the law of grace under which mankind presently sits, and teaching that would be a complete misappropriation of the Word. I do however want to draw attention to God's loving character that does act in a manner to bless us when we are active in faithful obedience to him,[248] but it should be underscored that the Word is also clear that action is the catalyst that results in blessings rather than the other way around. I can say this affirmatively because when I was younger, I errantly thought that I needed wait for the Lord to "do" something first, and only then would I be able to put forth the faithful action needed to fulfill his plan for my life. I had it backwards.

Please allow me to draw your attention to this author's emphasized word "if" in verse two above. It informs us that in God's economy, blessings can be conditional. This is affirmed by the apostle Paul in Galatians 6:7-8. The principle of reaping and sowing is a universal principle because it applies to both the righteous[249] and the unrighteous.[250] We must first *do* something to receive something. Activation is needed, and it only starts when we get our feet moving. God also informs us what those feet should be doing, for this information immediately follows the conditional term "if." We should "*obey the Lord your God.*" An additional component of this teaching can be found in Deuteronomy 28:12 since it tells us that God opens up heaven's storehouses to "bless the work of our hands."[251] Notice this verse implies that we are already in the process of working when the blessings are given. Far too many times I have been guilty of procrastinating to see what blessings God would give rather than just taking the bull by the horns, getting to work, and then experiencing the blessings he is willing to bestow. Perhaps you too have run into this "hedge of thorns?"[252] God's Word is clear that we need to be working on what God calls us to do, and it promises us that if and when we begin doing that, God will then bless our work.[253] When we find ourselves stalled in life and caught in this

---

247 Cf. Ephesian 2:8-9; Galatians 2:21; Romans 11:6; Acts 13:39 and Romans 3:20-30
248 Romans 4:1-7; https://www.biblegateway.com/passage/?search=Romans+4%3A1-7&version=NIV
249 Cf. Matthew 13:23
250 Cf. Hosea 8:7
251 https://biblehub.com/deuteronomy/28-12.htm
252 Proverbs 15:19; https://www.biblegateway.com/passage/?search=Proverbs+15%3A19&version=ESV
253 Cf. Proverbs 13:4, 10:4, 20:13, 14:23; James 4:17; Hebrews 12:11, 6:12

trap of possible laziness but certain disobedience, we need to ask ourselves two questions:

a. Are we obeying what God wants us to do?
b. What kind of work are we already doing that God can bless?

God is looking for people to bless.[254] II Chronicles 16:9 (The Message) makes this clear: "GOD is always on the alert, constantly on the lookout for people who are totally committed to him." What are you doing for the Lord? Are you committed to Him? Are you serving others, or are you looking for those who can best serve you and your interests? Are you renewing your mind in God's Word? These are questions we must all seriously answer if we truly seek to please the Lord and receive his blessings.

When I wanted to move from the classroom into a leadership position, I had to ask myself these same questions. I determined the answer to the first question was affirmed since I had entered the profession of education after running from it for a while. My goal was education leadership, so I was okay there. After sincerely considering the second question, I had to admit that I wasn't doing as much as I could have to be blessed by God with a leadership position, so I came to a moment where I had to make a decision. Do I sow extra actions of leadership in my school that God will be able to bless, or do I just wait for God to simply drop a leadership job into my lap? Reaping always starts with the obedience of sowing, not the other way around, so I figured I better not wait for that "drop" too long. We don't obey God only after he gives us something we desire, although he does sometimes bless us out of the graciousness of his character.[255] Through the time I spent assuming extra leadership duties, God chose to not only bless me later, he also blessed me through the work. During those times I was engaged in additional duties, God taught me selflessness. I discovered through action how to be a servant leader.[256] Once I learned this critical lesson of leadership, it was then that God placed me into education leadership, and I often tell people how much I want to be a "servant leader."

---

[254] Psalm 103:13, 145:9; 37:4; Jeremiah 29:11; Matthew 6:11
[255] Cf. John 1:16
[256] Cf. Matthew 20:26; Luke 22:26; Mark 10:43

In summary, when we learn that God operates by the principle of reaping and sowing in his own economy, we then are empowered to operate correctly according to his principles. Once we are functioning according to his principles, we are now in a place where God can bless us as well as the work we do. Give God something to bless. Show a proper attitude even when times are tough. Love others even when you feel betrayed. Forgive others who are not sorry for their hurtful actions. Bless those who have no intention of blessing you. These are all actions. I am not advising this because I have read it. I am shouting this to any who will hear because I have had to live right through this very process! Obey the Lord first, and then watch the storehouses of Heaven drop more blessings on you than you can imagine.

FINITE OBSTACLES

Laziness, Apathy, Complacency, Negligence

INFINITE TRUTH

Jesus was a man of action. We too need to emulate that action and allow God to bless our efforts to obey him.

PRAYER

Dear Lord, you are worthy of all praise, honor, and glory. Thank you for your Word and instruction. Please forgive us of our sins, and place us on the path of obedience to your Word. Reveal to us your will for our lives, and bless the obedience we do in response to your revelations. Bless the works of our hands. In the name of Jesus our Lord and Savior, amen.

Lesson 30

Strong People Are Forged By Strong Hands

"David noticed that his servants were whispering among themselves and he realized the child was dead. 'Is the child dead?' he asked. 'Yes,' they replied, 'he is dead.' Then David got up from the ground. After he had washed, put on lotions and changed his clothes, he went into the house of the LORD and worshiped. Then he went to his own house, and at his request they served him food, and he ate. His servants asked him, 'Why are you acting this way? While the child was alive, you fasted and wept, but now that the child is dead, you get up and eat!' He answered, 'While the child was still alive, I fasted and wept. I thought, 'Who knows? The LORD may be gracious to me and let the child live.' But now that

> *he is dead, why should I fast? Can I bring him back again? I will go to him, but he will not return to me'."*
>
> II SAMUEL 12:19-23

Most of us can look back at a specific period of time in our lives and identify a certain "storm" where the Lord used strong winds and choppy seas to drive home his loving lessons with spectacular impact. When I scrutinize the years between February 2003 through July 2005 in my own life, I cannot help but draw strength from the situation King David went through when his first son with Bathsheba was taken from him. During these aforementioned months, I went through the typical emotional rollercoaster that frequently accompanies divorce. Anyone who has experienced a similar event can attest that times like these are meant to forge character through all of the anguish, challenges, and faith-building seasons. When I finally accounted for all that was lost during this storm, I was able to list almost everything of earthly value. However, what I gained through the experience was of eternal value, and as each year goes by, I recognize the veracity of Joseph's words in Genesis 50:20.[257] While there are times in our lives where someone(s) intended to harm us, our sovereign God ensures that those events work out for good so that his will may be accomplished by what follows, and many times these events serve to save us and/or other people. If a person is ever able to conceptualize the infinite work God does through stormy times despite the inherent struggles, it builds faith in God due to the realization that the struggles yield a permanent positive(s) in our lives.

It would be both easy and currently popular to declare victimhood, but I would be amiss if I did. While I lost a son during that storm, I ended up gaining literally hundreds of other children who I now influence as an educator. The impact and guidance that educators have on young people often are life-changing, and I imagine everyone reading this book can think back to a particular educator who helped positively shape their lives forever. I did not at first recognize this, but through experience, I am now able to confirm

---

[257] "You intended to harm me, but God intended it for good to accomplish what is now being done, the saving of many lives." https://www.biblehub.com/genesis/50-20.htm

William Cowper's hymn that the Lord does work in mysterious ways.[258] I can now also affirm that Deuteronomy 8:5, Proverbs 3:11-12 and Hebrews 12:6 are veritable statements: Because God loves me, he used a period of time in my life to cultivate, shape, and direct me toward his will for my life as an educator. Due to my experiences, I can now relate with the numerous children and adults I encounter who experience various forms of trauma in their lives, and the relationships that can be built when people have encountered similar experiences is so much stronger than one where there is no common ground. Since God comforted me through pain, I too can now comfort and assist many through their pain just as II Corinthians 1:3-8 teaches us. God also used this experience to confirm within my heart that he does indeed love me, because he did chastise me and he declares he only does that to those he loves.[259] God also began to reveal a more complete picture of himself to me through this encounter. Deuteronomy 3:24 declares, "O Sovereign LORD, you have begun to show to your servant your greatness and your **strong hand**. For what god is there in heaven or on earth who can do the deeds and mighty works you do? (Emphasis the author's)." God's hand was "strong" in different ways as he shaped me, but I now thank God for that treatment for it forged a strong man as a result.

You may be wondering what it was that God needed to change in me that required such a strong hand? I was guilty of idolatry for many years even though I was a Christian. In fact, one could argue that I was a polytheist, and it was not intentional on my part yet still true. I did love God, but I also loved other things that became idols in my life as well. Thankfully, the Lord loved me far too much to let me to stay in that predicament and I am now confident that he began a good work in my life and is currently working to complete it.[260] God had to refine my life through "fire" in order to bring about the purity he desires for me, which is why I argue that I am not a victim. I once heard author and speaker Morris Morrison state that he too had a tragic past, but he followed that up with a profound statement. He commented at a speaking engagement in which I attended, "I had a tough childhood, but that is not what I focus on." Hearing him say that statement was life-changing for me. His sagacious and

---

258 To gain more background on William Cowper's background that led him to pen this famous hymn, see Colleen Toole's brief historical piece located at https://www.umcdiscipleship.org/resources/history-of-hymns-god-moves-in-a-mysterious-way-cowper.
259 Cf. Proverbs 3:12; Hebrews 12:6
260 Cf. Philippians 1:6

insightful comment reveals incredible spiritual strength and Godly maturity. We may go through terrible events in our lives, but we do not have to focus on them. We instead should focus on our calling and simply recognize the pains we suffered in our past were "God's strong hands" conforming us to the image of his son.[261] Once we are able to do this, it is then that we truly understand that God does undoubtedly work in mysterious ways yet his ways radically change us and prepare us to bear good fruit for his glory.

I now want to tie-in the focal verses above from the book of II Samuel. Many of you may know the story of King David and Bathsheba. For those of you unfamiliar with the story, it can be read in II Samuel chapters eleven and twelve. In a nutshell, David was king over Israel and at the time of this story, he should have been leading his troops in battle. He wasn't however, and one day he saw one of his soldier's wives (Bathsheba) nakedly bathing and he lusted after her. David lusted so much that he acted upon that lust and went to Bathsheba's home and had an affair with her. As a result, she became pregnant. David attempted to cover up his sin by having Bathsheba's husband killed in battle, so David compounded his sin of adultery with the sin of murder. Bathsheba bore a son, but God's judgment for David's sin fell upon the child instead of the king and his mistress. While there are numerous lessons to be learned from this story, I would argue that the decisive lesson is the mysterious way that God used this tragic event to demonstrate the genius of his righteous and "strong hand."

First of all, consider the irony and foreshadowing of this Davidic situation: God chose to allow a son to die in lieu of the people who deserved to die as payment for their sin. David's unnamed son died when David and Bathsheba should have died, but out of God's mercy, he spared the lives of the parents. By God's sparing of their lives, the wisest man not named Jesus to ever walk to planet was born through them...King Solomon. Solomon was used by God to expand the kingdom of Israel. He reigned during Israel's most peaceful years, and he wrote two books of the Bible and contributed many statements to the book of Proverbs. Furthermore, it is through his genetic line that Jesus was born.[262] Jesus was also a son who was allowed to die in place of sinners, except he died for not just two people, but for all of mankind. It is through him that

---

261 Cf. Romans 8:29
262 Cf. Matthew 1:1-17

our sins are washed away should we accept his final payment and place him on the throne of our lives.

Secondly, these verses teach us that we need to trust God in our failures in life. David failed God, himself, and his nation miserably when he chose to stay home instead of going to battle with the rest of his soldiers. By remaining home, this resulted in his affair with Bathsheba. However, he did not disappoint God. In fact, we can't disappoint God because in order for a person to disappoint another, the person we disappoint has to have higher expectations for that person in order to be let down. Since God is omniscient and knows the past, present, and future, he already knows what is going to happen and has a perfect understanding of what to expect from us. He has already declared what we are like in Psalm 14:2-3:

The LORD looks down from heaven on the sons of men to see if there are any who understand, any who seek God. All have turned aside, they have together become corrupt; there is no one who does good, not even one.

God already knows that we are contemptible and we therefore cannot disappoint him.[263] We do not disappoint God when we sin, for we are not powerful enough to prevent God's plans for us from being realized.[264] Yes, we sin and have to face the consequences of that sin because God is just, but God's grace does not hold disappointment against us like we humans do to each other.[265] We hope in Christ, not the other way around. God knows that we fall short of his glory,[266] and he takes the remaining ashes left after we sin and turns them into something sublime.[267] David failed miserably, but he still trusted God after this event. In yet another mysterious act of our loving God, he gave the same man who sinned and lost a son another son who became a king in the lineage of Christ!

---

[263] For more information concerning this topic, consider how Jesus called out Peter just before the crucifixion, declaring that Peter would deny him three times before sunrise. That certainly would have disappointed many of us, but when we read Mark 16:6-7, we see the angel at the tomb tell Mary Magdalene, Mary, and Salome to "go tell the disciples *and Peter*" that they will meet Jesus in Galilee. God had his angel again call out Peter in a reassuring manner to let him and us know that Jesus was not disappointed with him.
[264] Cf. Job 42:2
[265] Cf. II Corinthians 12:19
[266] Cf. Romans 3:23
[267] Cf. Isaiah 61:1-3

Thirdly, we need to understand that God tests us frequently. James 1:2-4 tell us to:

Consider it pure joy, my brothers, whenever you face trials of many kinds, because you know that the testing of your faith develops perseverance. Perseverance must finish its work so that you may be mature and complete, not lacking anything.

God's tests are to help us develop. Children get tested in school as they are being taught the lessons of curriculum and life, and God too tests us to help us mature in Christ. As parents and teachers, we strive to rear strong children who can live productive lives. God also desires strong Christians who can fulfill his will by leading productive lives that bear fruit for his kingdom.

Additionally, we need to understand that God sometimes disciplines us when we do step out of line in order to make our circumstances so tough that we don't repeat our failures. It is true that we often fall back into our sinful ways after initial chastisement, but I have discovered that when God has to give a "make-up test," such tests tend to be harder than the original one. Due to our sin-natures, we will inevitably take multiple make-up tests in life, but we can be assured that God loves us enough to purify us through fire in order to bring us to holiness[268] through these tests. We should always strive to ace God's tests the first time, and the only way that can occur is to be in God's Word on a daily basis in order to learn and understand his will. We also need to develop a consistent and daily prayer life in order to keep the lines of communication with God open so that we can be guided by the Holy Spirit. And lastly, we need to trust Jesus that he will accomplish in our lives that which he set out to do. We do this through a faithful walk, understanding that the Christian life is a marathon and not a sprint.[269]

Finally, we need to understand how and why David responded to the death of his son. His actions shocked his servants, but we too should behave in a manner that "shocks the world" when it witnesses tragedy in our lives. David mourned and fasted while his son was dying but got up, cleaned and

---

268 Cf. Hebrews 12:9-11
269 Cf. I Corinthians 9:23-25

anointed himself, ate, and went to war (got back to work) after his son died. His servants did not realize why he wasn't mournful when his son died, and David responded that it was because he could not bring his son back from the dead. He had beseeched God to change his mind while his son was still alive, but once God allowed the death to occur, David understood God's justice enough that he accepted God's will and moved forward with his calling. That is a lesson that took me two and a half years to learn, and while I miss my beloved son, I know he is still alive and I pray that God will one day reunite us. I also trust God that he knew what he was doing when he allowed our separation to occur. I also know God is a just God and will righteously make the matter right but in his timing, not mine. Perhaps the real lesson in all of this is that God does not want us to pout about the negatives and failures in our lives. God simply wants us to trust his strong hand, draw closer to him, and allow him to create holiness in our lives through running a race that develops spiritual maturity through difficult tests through which he puts us.

Just as our own children have to learn to take responsibility in their own lives, God also expects us to become responsible Christians. One aspect of responsibility involves learning to allow God's tests, our failures, and bad circumstances in life not to steal our joy. The joy of the Lord is our strength,[270] and I had to keep telling this to myself for a long time before I conceptualized this truth. Even when bad things happen to us, we should allow the joy of God to solidify our footing in life. It is time for us to do the will of God just as David did when he got up and went to war. When we allow God's strong hand to result in pity-parties for ourselves, this only disgraces the work of Jesus, shames ourselves, and is just one more test we fail that will require a make-up test.

---

270 Cf. Nehemiah 8:10

FINITE OBSTACLES

A myopic understanding of how God uses trials to shape and strengthen us. Self-pity, ungodly anger towards God, Bitterness

INFINITE TRUTH

God loves us enough to lead us through hard life-lessons in order to forge strong Christians who can be used for his will and glory. Failure to see difficulties in this manner tend to leave us bitter and resentful instead of approachable and gracious.

PRAYER

Dear Lord, please strike from us any shameful self-pity we have in our lives. Remove from us the spiritual ineptitude that plagues so many of us from fulfilling your will and receiving the blessings you have in store for our lives. Direct us in your will to meet the needs of those you have placed in our lives, and give us the strength and courage to finish the race you set before us. In the name of our loving savior, Jesus, amen.

LESSON 31

CHOOSE FRIENDS, NOT DESERT ISOLATION

> *"Elijah was afraid and ran for his life. When he came to Beersheba in Judah, he left his servant there, while he himself went a day's journey into the desert. He came to a broom tree, sat down under it and prayed that he might die. 'I have had enough, LORD,' he said. 'Take my life; I am no better than my ancestors'."* (Emphasis the author's)
>
> I KINGS 19:3-4

I really enjoy watching the old Clint Eastwood westerns. One of my particular favorites of his is *The Outlaw Josey Wales*. In this movie, the set of which takes place in the 19th century shortly after the end of the American Civil War, Eastwood's character "Josey Wales" ends up moving west with a small group of people and runs into a hostile tribe of Indians. In one of the scenes where the viewer first encounters the Indians, Eastwood and his cadre find themselves in a valley with the potentially dangerous Indians up on the hills looking down upon them. The atmosphere the movie imparts upon the viewer during these moments is one of fear and a feeling of hopelessness. The Indians could have easily attacked the itinerants victoriously because they occupied the higher ground and had the advantage in numbers. Of course the star of the film later meets with the Indian chief and manages to work things out with his tribe, but my point is that the group of western expansionists were vulnerable to easy attack because they were in a valley and isolated. How many times have we placed ourselves in such a hypothetical situation where we can easily be attacked by Satan's minions?

Elijah was one of the major prophets in scripture, and a review of the Old Testament will reveal he was a man through which God demonstrated much of his divine power. Elijah's anointing by God was so special that he is only one of two known men to never have tasted physical death yet.[271] Based on the Biblical record, Elijah was a mighty man of God who witnessed many feats of miraculous interjection by God into the physical world, yet Elijah's stories also reveal to us that even the mightiest men (and women) of faith can succumb to their humanity. One of the blessings of God's Word is the fact that it does not attempt to paint a perfect picture within its record. It shows men and women in their naturally flawed states, and we can therefore relate to mighty heroes of the faith because we see them just as dysfunctional, sometimes as cynical, and typically as fragile as we are.

This mighty prophet of God, a man who God used to call fire down from heaven to burn up a water-soaked sacrifice,[272] actually left his friends behind and ran for his life when threatened by Queen Jezebel. Elijah was scared, not trusting God, and his eyes were on his circumstances instead of God. Even though Elijah was an intrepid prophet, he was still a human prophet who made a wrong choice. Instead of allowing God to work through those who the Lord had placed in his life, Elijah seems to have instead went out to think on his own in order to try and work out his own problems. After capitulating to his feelings of being overwhelmed and doomed, he actually prayed that God take

---

[271] Contrast II Kings 2:11 with Revelation 11:7 while keeping in mind Hebrews 9:27 informs us that "it is appointed unto men once to die, but after this the judgment:"
[272] Cf. I Kings 18:37-38

his life. Astonishingly, he did this *the day after* his mountain-top experience where God enabled him to humiliate and then defeat Jezebel's prophets of Baal!

Once we arrive at a point of failure in our lives, this is when the devil has the advantage to attack us. He is an accuser[273] and likes to kick us when we are down. We are especially vulnerable in a valley when we isolate ourselves. Satan hunts "like a roaring lion,"[274] and any viewing of a National Geographic television show about lions typically shows how they always isolate and then attack weak prey. When we feel spiritually defeated, this can become a time where we look to flee our problems and attempt to figure out solutions on our own. This is a mistake, however. We instead have to look to God for strength[275] and sustenance, for we know God faithfully meets the needs of his children.[276] When we feel tempted to isolate ourselves out of fear, this may be a time God wants you to lean on a friend[277] for support. The apostle Paul informs us that we are not unaware of Satan's schemes,[278] so when Satan inevitably does attack you, you already know his strategy.

Why is it that when we get into the valleys of life we humans tend to focus on ourselves and our problems instead of the God who has saved us and promised never to forsake us as we progress through every event in our lives? Why is it that we often isolate ourselves and "leave our servant (friends) behind" and go into a metaphorical desert by ourselves? How many times have we had a bad day, come home and gone into our rooms, turned on the television or a video game and tried to escape this life's problems? How many of us have turned to addictions of all sorts to numb our pain or ease our worries? What is going to speak truth into our lives when we are in a valley...the secular humanistic television and gaming programs or holy God? How many video games or television programs speak words of Biblical truth to you through their messages? How many times has God used those he has placed in your life to speak Biblical words of truth to you? How many times has God himself spoken words of truth to you when you ran to him in prayer and through scripture reading?

---

273 Cf. Zechariah 3:1-2; Job 2:1-6; Revelation 12:10
274 I Peter 5:8; https://biblehub.com/1_peter/5-8.htm
275 Cf. Psalm 105:4
276 Philippians 4:19; https://biblehub.com/philippians/4-19.htm
277 Cf. Galatians 6:2 and Hebrews 13:16
278 II Corinthians 2:11; https://www.biblehub.com/2_corinthians/2-11.htm

If we can ever arrive at a humble point in our lives where objective and honest introspection can occur, we likely will find that we succumb to our humanity many times. Because I have experienced great "mountain-top" moments of spiritual success in my life only to be followed by "valley" moments of failure, I know how Elijah felt. Because I have gone from a high point to a low point in life and ran from my problems, I know the embarrassment that Elijah likely felt once God decided to confront his cowardice. Because God chose to record Elijah's low points in scripture, I am also thankful that this passage reveals to us that even the strongest of faith fail. God gives us this story to show us that it is not uncommon, nor is it wise to isolate ourselves while attempting to flee the threats we encounter in life. I can rest better knowing that even the greatest Biblical characters failed miserably, so when I also fail, I can look to the below scriptures and know God has brought people into my life to help me overcome my challenges by the power of the Holy Spirit.

Ecclesiastes 4:9 and 12 tell us that "Two are better than one..." and "Though one may be overpowered, two can defend themselves." God has placed people in our lives so that he might sometimes work his will through them. We have spouses, families, friends, and even strangers who can team with us so that we better defend ourselves. God can and sometimes does speak truth into our lives during our valley experiences through others. When we are isolated, that is exactly the time we need someone to tell us God's truths.

Ecclesiastes 6:10 tells us that "...no man can contend with one who is stronger than he." We cannot defend ourselves against Satan without the Holy Spirit. He is simply too overpowering for humans. However, thanks be to God that "Greater is he that is in me (the Holy Spirit) than he that is of the world (Satan)."[279] We often try to work out our problems on our own but should instead immerse ourselves into the Bible so that God can speak truth to our hearts and provide the power to overcome Satan. Get into the Word of God and begin praying every day if you do not already. Not doing so leaves us vulnerable to being overwhelmed by our adversaries.

Lastly, Psalm 73 is a poem from Asaph who was a prominent musician for Israelite Kings David and Solomon.[280] The entirety of this chapter is Asaph reflecting back on how he almost screwed up in life by removing his focus

---

279 I John 4:4; https://www.biblehub.com/1_john/4-4.htm
280 See: https://www.biblegateway.com/resources/encyclopedia-of-the-bible/Asaph

from God and onto his personal problems. Verse sixteen declares that he tried to "go it alone," but he acknowledges that doing so "was oppressive to (him)." He then admits that the solution to his problems only became clear when he "entered the sanctuary of God" and was then able to "gain understanding."

Folks, we cannot operate safely by ourselves. We cannot make it through life alone. Even the very first man (Adam) who was made in God's very image was not left alone by God but was instead brought a wife to complete him. Even the apostle Paul, who wished people could remain unmarried like him, still had many friends upon which he relied throughout his life. God has placed people in our lives to help us and, likewise, he has placed us in others' lives to help them. God cared for us deeply enough that he allowed his own son to be brutally killed so that we might have fellowship with him. Don't run to isolation when you have had a bad day. Run to the Lord first in prayer. He may then have you discuss your problems with those close to your lives so that they can comfort you with the comfort they too have received.[281] We have no idea what God may have been communicating to our friends each day. Maybe God gave your spouse a word for you that day. Maybe God has burdened a trusted friend to pray for you this past week while also allowing a crisis to occur in your life so that the two of you could meet and discuss what God laid on your friend's heart. It may be hard not to "leave your friend" and "journey into the desert," but the Lord has given us people to assist us through our valleys. We would be wise not to isolate ourselves.

FINITE OBSTACLES

Self-isolation, Fear, Intimidation, Thinking we can be a "Lone Ranger" and live a successful life.

INFINITE TRUTH

Many times, God will use people to accomplish his will. He loves mankind enough to use them in his master plan. This is why he calls us to fellowship with others.

---

[281] II Corinthians 1:4; https://www.biblehub.com/2_corinthians/1-4.htm

PRAYER

Dear Lord, thank you for the honesty your Word reveals to us about our flawed human nature. Thank you for giving us examples in the Bible of great people who greatly failed in life. Thank you that you are our rock and salvation. I humbly ask you to forgive us for isolating ourselves when we have problems instead of seeking your will and understanding. Please allow your word to sink into our hearts and sear our hearts so that we become warriors for you. Teach us to run to you and our friends instead of to our "deserts." Teach us to allow our spouses, families, and friends to communicate your will to us as well. Place in us a spirit of discernment so that when our valley experiences arrive we are able to recognize Satan's traps and avoid them. In the name of Jesus, amen.

Epilogue

I stated at the outset that the reason I have written this book is an attempt to share some of the lessons I have learned in life with the masses in an effort to help convey God's infinite truths to anyone willing to read or hear them. I believe very strongly that Jesus Christ is the only hope for a troubled world made up of troubled people who all deal with a sin-nature that causes each of us to lose sight of truth. When I painted the Latin phrase *"Veritas Lux Mea"* above my classroom door, I did so with purpose. I wanted the students, parents, and educators who entered my classroom to know that the common term of "truth" has uncommon power to radically change the world. I sought for my students to focus on truth as their guiding light, knowing that if I could entice them to develop a love for truth, their life-long effort of searching for it would yield critically-thinking people who have the capacity for making wise decisions. I also knew that a developed hunger for truth would ultimately drive my students toward the ultimate source of truth, Jesus Christ. John 14:6 is a record of Jesus telling the world that he is "the way and the truth and the life. No one comes to the Father except through (him)." We can therefore conclude that Jesus *is* truth, and that allows us to replace the term "Veritas" in my phrase with the Latin term for Christ, *"Christos."* When I use the term "Christos" synonymously in place of "Veritas," that phrase then conveys the idea that "Christ Enlightens Me."

True enlightenment then always points back to Jesus Christ, and since enlightenment always comes from a conceptualization of truth, learning in and of itself then has to point back to Jesus Christ. This is why I based this book on Proverbs 1:7. As I am an educator, commissioned by a state authority to take our greatest resource (children) and equip them to be educated, life-long learners who utilize learned critical thinking skills to contribute both wisely and positively to their families, their communities, and this great nation, I would not be fulfilling my commission if I did not help them understand that each one of them has the highest of callings to develop their minds correctly. By law, I am prohibited from telling students what to think, and I am very diligent to uphold the law. However, by commission, I have to convey to students the idea that they *must* learn to think, and in order to achieve accurate thoughts, they have to base those thoughts on accurate information. Accurate information is commonly called "facts," and facts are indeed truth. Since God tells us the he is truth, we can then conclude that what Christ teaches must be factual. And if what Christ teaches is factual, it then behooves us to know what he taught so that we can make wise decisions based on truth. Such wise decisions based on truth were once identified as "Common Sense."

Common sense is no longer common because we have allowed ourselves to become foolish. Proverbs 1:7 declares, "The fear of the Lord is the beginning of knowledge, but fools despise wisdom and instruction." When America began to corporately turn its back on the reverence of God, we ensured that a lack of knowledge would become common. Since the knowledge we learn and teach to others became devoid of wisdom and instruction, we ultimately began conveying platitudes and pithy statements in place of good sense. As more and more of the masses accepted these pithy platitudes as knowledge, we lost the ability to think objectively and critically because our focus was now on the unstable foundation of opinion rather than rock-solid truth.

Since I posit in this book that "common sense is no longer common," I essentially am declaring that it is no longer common to witness people make wise decisions based on truth. How do we change that? We have to get back to truth. The thirty-one lessons discussed in this book are just a compilation of lessons I have had to learn the "hard way," but I ensure each one of them is tied to the truth found in the Word of God. Most of us learn well when we hear stories that we can relate to. I attempted to share some of my stories with my readers with the hopes that they may learn that without the correct outlook on this world, we are very likely to miss the wisdom that can be learned while we walk through it. I am an educator. My goal is to always teach. I was graciously called to the truth by Christ despite the fact that I was a sinner by birth into the human race. Now that I have been exposed to truth, I have a responsibility to teach what I learn to people. I know for a fact that "truth enlightens" all of us, and if I can contribute to society just one book that turns a person toward the truth of the Lord Jesus Christ, I have taught well. If I can convince people that there is a grander "infinite war" going on for their minds, I have enlightened them unto wisdom. If I can teach a person that the "finite wars" they focus on in their daily lives can be fought with the eternal and infinite wisdom of God, I have lead them to truth. If I can lead someone to Christ with this book, I have fulfilled my 'Great Commission[282]" as a Christian. And if America would ever get back to the truth that enlightens them, we would start seeing common sense become common again, and our nation and those around us could again benefit from the application of good decisions commonly made on a daily basis while at the same time again reap the blessings of God.

---

282 Cf. Matthew 28:16-20

www.ingramcontent.com/pod-product-compliance
Lightning Source LLC
Chambersburg PA
CBHW011233160426
43209CB00041B/1985/J